KU-525-987

Melon Revised

and

TARTUFFE:
An Adaptation

SIMON GRAY

faber and faber
LONDON · BOSTON

First published in 1990
by Faber and Faber Limited
Queen Square, London WC1N 3AU

Photoset by Parker Typesetting Service Leicester
Printed in Great Britain by
Cox and Wyman Ltd Reading

© Simon Gray, 1990

A CIP record for this book is
available from the British Library.

ISBN 0–571–14240–0

THE HOLY TERROR:
Melon Revised

and

TARTUFFE:
An Adaptation

SIMON GRAY

faber and faber
LONDON · BOSTON

First published in 1990
by Faber and Faber Limited
3 Queen Square, London WC1N 3AU

Photoset by Parker Typesetting Service Leicester
Printed in Great Britain by
Cox and Wyman Ltd Reading

© Simon Gray, 1990

All professional and amateur rights are strictly
reserved and applications to perform them must
be made in writing to Judy Daish, 83 Eastbourne
Mews, London W2 6LQ.

A CIP record for this book is
available from the British Library.

ISBN 0-571-14240-0

CONTENTS

The first version of this play, called *Melon*, was first produced at the Haymarket Theatre, London, and ran for six months with Alan Bates in the lead. It was provoked by Professor Stuart Sutherland's *Breakdown*, an honourably ruthless autobiographical account of a prolonged emotional and mental collapse. The catalyst of the collapse seemed to be Professor Sutherland's sudden and uncontrollable jealousy, provoked by his wife's long-standing infidelity, an infidelity that Professor Sutherland had initially encouraged, while himself engaging in a series of feckless, and frequently boasted-about, short-term affairs. In other words, it was an account – or seemed to be – of a married man driven mad by the consequences of his own cavalier sexual behaviour, and then driven further mad by the damage his madness inflicted on his marriage. A perfectly vicious circle. When I came to write this play those seemed to me the dramatically serviceable facts, and I set about organizing them in very different terms, for my own ends. Melon himself, a flamboyantly aggressive publisher, probably had little in common with the dry-toned experimental psychologist of *Breakdown*; Melon's wife, his circle of friends, his professional colleagues, above all the post 'cure' in-bursts and out-bursts of an obsessed memory, were all theatrical inventions for which no evidence was provided in the book.

The play was written during a brief period when I'd replaced heavy smoking with a stomach-corrupting nicotine chewing-gum. I have at times suspected that these processes of simultaneous withdrawal and addiction contributed to the lunatic organization of the piece. At any rate, once I was back on cigarettes, I had trouble (the only time in my life) in recognizing the work on the stage as mine. No fault of either the excellent cast, or of the devoted and gifted director, who were all completely faithful to the text. It was just that there grew – through try-outs at Guildford, Bath, Richmond, through its successful run in London – a conviction that I'd got something wrong. Perhaps simply that the connections were too logical: an open marriage provoking jealousy; jealousy leading to madness; madness destroying everything of value in the marriage. My first uneasiness was followed by a growing recognition of certain structural deficiencies – in particular, a nightmare sequence in the second act that came more and more to seem a vaudeville set piece that fatally interrupted the narrative flow. And then bits of this scene here, that scene there, that I couldn't, however hard I tried, quite accept.

About six months ago I decided to look at the play again – 'to try to get it right' was the phrase I remember using. My intention, even so, was only to replace the nightmare scene with something more narratively cohering, and then do a bit of patchwork around and about the place. Instead I found myself starting from the beginning, writing the whole play through again and again, until I eventually lost contact, not only with the Haymarket version, but also with the central premise in Professor Sutherland's book that had made me want to write the play in the first place, but in which, I now realized, I'd never truly believed: that jealousy can induce the kind of madness that requires institutionalization, drugs, electro-convulsive therapy. Exactly the reverse now seemed to me more likely to be true – that so serious an illness could well have jealousy as its first and major *symptom*. The new succession of drafts flowed from that realization, and the last draft, published here, amounts to a new play, with not a single scene, and scarcely more than a dozen lines, left over from the Haymarket version. New characters have come into being, old ones have reduced or altered themselves, Melon has even found a new, and specific, audience to address, with whom he is, I hope, more at home than with his previous, anonymous one.

It's not for me to say whether the new play is better or worse – or *even* worse – than the old one. But what I can say with confidence is that I am much happier with it, and would prefer to have it accepted as the authentic, if not the final version (that will have to wait until after its first production). It's no corroboration of my own conviction of the greater truthfulness of this work, I know, to add that while I was working on it Professor Sutherland produced a new edition of *Breakdown* in which he included a new chapter describing a ghastly recurrence of his illness. This time his relationship with his wife (they'd separated; she'd remarried) played no part. His conclusion was that both breakdowns were inevitable, whatever his marital circumstances, and that the initial jealousy was therefore a symptom, not a cause.

The first production of *The Holy Terror* was broadcast on BBC Radio 3 in October 1989. The first stage production is scheduled for New York in the autumn of 1990.

The version of *Tartuffe* included in this volume was commissioned by the Kennedy Center, Washington, and performed in May 1982. My impertinent intention in undertaking it was to find, if such a thing were there to be found, a completely English play that could pass under the original title, set in the original social and historical context. The Englishness of it was therefore a matter of the psychology and, of course, the expression. The first entailed the transformation of some of the characters in order that I, at least, should understand why they behave as they do. The second, which followed from the first, entailed that the characters should speak in a language that expressed the needs and fears of their natures as I understood them. All English verse translations of Molière have always struck me as ultimately tedious, even when accomplished and agile, if only because the French alexandrine is as free (the possibilities of rhyme in French being virtually endless) as the English heroic couplet is constricted. In Molière's alexandrines we hear the characters in much the same way that we hear the characters in Shakespeare's blank verse. In, for instance, Richard Wilbur's and Tony Harrison's translations of Molière we mostly hear the poet's skill in pulling off unlikely rhymes in order to avoid the likely ones. After a time, whoever the character, whatever the dramatic urgencies, we seem to hear only the same skilful voice.

But really I make no apology for having a go – or making a stab – at *Tartuffe*. However much I might damage my own reputation, I'm unlikely to damage Molière's.

SIMON GRAY

THE HOLY TERROR
Melon Revised

The Holy Terror: Melon Revised was first performed on BBC Radio 3 in October 1989.

The cast included:

MARK MELON	James Laurenson
GLADSTONE	Robin Bailey
SAMANTHA	Susie Brann
MICHAEL	Sylvester Morand
JACOB	Brian Miller
RUPERT	Struan Rodger
GRAEME	Joe Dunlop
JOSH MELON	Samuel West
GLADYS POWERS	Joan Walker
KATE MELON	Marcia King
SHRINK	Geoffrey Whitehead

ACT ONE

MELON: Ms. Um, chairperson, ladies and – well, ladies, eh.
(*Little laugh*) First I am under instruction to tell you not to
worry. When your delightful Mrs Macdonald told me of the
tradition of your tea-break, a tradition far more honoured in
the observing than in the breach, as Mrs Macdonald wittily
put it, I decided to play absolutely safe by bringing along this
rather natty little alarm clock – a recent birthday present
from someone – someone very dear to me – and I've set it to
go off at four fifteen precisely. So don't be alarmed by the
alarm, eh, it's rather loud and piercing, and rush for the exits
thinking there's a fire or some such. Rush to the exits by all
means, but only for your tea and sandwiches. There. We've
got almost the most important thing out of the way, haven't
we? But I hope that the rest of what I say won't just be a way
of filling time until the tea and sandwiches, oh, and cakes,
too – I know, as Mrs Macdonald allowed me a little peep at
them on the way in, what a scrumptious selection – but even
so, with those in prospect, I hope I'll be able to say
something interesting about my life and times as a publisher.
A little warning here, though, ladies. I'm not one for formal
addresses, carefully structured and skilfully organized and
meticulously rehearsed. All I've got to keep me on the
straight and narrow, so to speak, are a few notes on a few
cards, so that when I'm in danger of getting lost, or even
worse losing you, I can furnish myself with a little signpost
and so point my nose back towards you, here in Chichester.
Cheltenham, that is. So sorry, ladies. If I sometimes confuse
them in my mind, it's not only because they sound the same,
and they share a tranquillity, a charm, a peacefulness that is
balm to the turbulent soul – so indeed I felt this morning,
when I got off the train and treated myself to a little stroll
along the leafy avenues. Such a relief from the broil and
moil, the lunacy – (*Stops, stares out*) um, chaos of London

3

life. (*Stops again*.) Time for a card, me thinks, eh? (*Little laugh*.) But where are they? I had them here. In my hand. I know I did. (*Looking around, then gropes in pocket*.) Ah yes. Here we are. Card number one. 'Say sorry.' Say sorry? But what for? I haven't said anything to say sorry for yet, have I? Oh, it must be to apologize in advance for some of the things I might suddenly find myself saying. Yes, indeed. That's it – it must be. Because I've discovered from recent experience that one of the dangers of a free-wheeling style is that certain matters tend to bob up by association, so to speak, that may be quite relevant – so I'm not talking about getting lost here – quite relevant, in fact of the utmost relevance, but nevertheless a trifle – a trifle unexpected. By being rather personal. So if I should suddenly find myself suddenly describing myself as behaving like a Hashemite widow, as I've been known to do when speaking publicly – known to describe myself, I mean, not actually *behave* like a Hashemite widow – good heavens, I hope not, no, no, that sort of thing is all very much in the past – I'm not actually sure, now that I've spoken the words, that I know what a Hashemite is, by the way. Do any of you ladies know what a Hashemite is? Oh, well, never mind. I'm sure we can all imagine how his widow would behave, can't we? (*Laughs*) Gosh, I feel comfortable! Here in this room with so many kind and interested ladies – at least you look interested, thank you for that – there was a time, you know, and not so long ago either, when I would have laughed aloud at the thought of standing here in front of you today. Yes, I would not only have thrown an invitation to address the Chichester (*Raises a finger*) – Cheltenham Women's Institute straight into the wastepaper basket, but I'd have made a bawdy joke or two in the bargain. You can guess the sort of thing. Well, I can tell you, ladies, not any more. Things have changed. It's not my habit these days to make jokes about women, or indeed about sex. There seems to me nothing funny to be found in either. So never fear, ladies, you won't be getting any bawdiness from me! But now you're probably saying to yourself, 'Oh, I do wish the silly fellow

would stop telling us what he's not going to tell us, and just get on with it and tell us what he is going to tell us.' And if you're not, it's only because you're too kind and patient. So why don't I just leap in and – and – now where did I intend to start? (*Looks at card*) Oh, yes. 'Conquering all before me.' Oh, well, perhaps I shouldn't have read that aloud, it sounds so immodest, doesn't it? But the truth is, ladies, it's the truth. When I was invited to an interview by Mr Gladstone, of Harkness and Gladstone, I was approaching the peak of my powers at Haylife and Forling. I was the youngest managing editor in London. And one of the most successful. I'd turned Haylife and Forling around in two years. Two years. The fact is, ladies, I already had a reputation as a whizz-kid and the *enfant terrible* of publishing. I was in demand!
(*Lights up on* GLADSTONE, *sitting at what is to become Melon's desk. He is partially deaf.* MELON, *bursting with energy, strides over, sits down.*)

MELON: Right. You play your cards, Edward. Then I'll play mine.

GLADSTONE: Well, as I'm sure you understand, Mark, what we want above all is to maintain our reputation as a great publishing house with great traditions.

MELON: Presumably you also wish to remain solvent.

GLADSTONE: (*After a small pause*) Our economic difficulties won't, I hope, lead us into pursuing current trends and fads –

MELON: In other words, you'd prefer not to move with the times.

GLADSTONE: With the times, yes. Certainly with the times. But the values that made us what we are –

MELON: Were.

GLADSTONE: Mmmm?

MELON: What you were, Edward. You aren't any longer what you were. What you are is nearly bankrupt. Or you wouldn't have sent for me, would you?

GLADSTONE: We have the greatest respect for all that you've done at Haylife and Forling. Who were, though of course in a less distinguished way, having a less distinguished list –

MELON: In less of a pickle than you are.

GLADSTONE: (*After a little pause*) Some of our finest literary
adornments are still alive and kicking. The great excitement
of the moment is that Agnes Merrivale has just delivered her
latest.

(*Looks expectantly at* MELON. MELON *says nothing.*)

We think very highly of it. Very highly indeed. Almost as
highly as Agnes does. (*Little laugh*) She used to be Arnold's
special concern, of course. I know I'm not breaking any
confidences when I tell you that they were lovers for a few
months during the war. When he was an air-raid warden,
you know, she'd join him on the roof and they'd watch the
V-2s falling all over London; Arnold said that the irony of it
was that he found it very exhilarating, he came to associate
his moments of amorous fulfilment with exploding rockets,
which is, I've often thought, why he and Muriel went
through a rather poor patch in their marriage just after he
and Agnes decided to be practical, or rather Arnold decided
to be practical. Now she'll have to come to me. Alas, I have
none of Arnold's gifts as an editor. Not that Agnes will need
too much editing.

MELON: Yes, well, I think we've at last raised the crucial
question, Edward. I'll have to have complete control. That
means editorially, too, needless to say.

GLADSTONE: (*After a small pause*) We do have a board. It's
written into our constitution, so to speak. And like Arnold
with Agnes, all the editors have their little pets.

MELON: You'll go under in two years – possibly eighteen
months – unless you do something very quickly. The quickest
thing you can do is to take me on as a full partner. In order to
do that, you have to give me editorial control. I shan't mind
the board meeting regularly to hear, approve and endorse my
decisions, as long as it doesn't take up too much of my time.

GLADSTONE: I'm not sure how the other, at least the senior,
editors will respond to that.

MELON: It won't matter much. As most of them won't be with us
if I come in.

GLADSTONE: My only wish, you know, speaking personally, is to relinquish the reins, retire to Arnold's little attic at the top of the building, and begin work on collating his memoirs. If you had any idea of what I have found up there! Letters from Ezra Pound, Tom Eliot, even Yeats – yes, even Yeats –

MELON: (*Cutting across*) I'd like to begin recruiting immediately. My own editors. Secretaries and so forth.

(GLADSTONE *sits nodding, as though in a daze.*)

So bugger off, Edward. Up to your attic. And let me get on with it, will you?

GLADSTONE: Well then – perhaps the best thing is for me to – well, let you get on with it, Mark. (*Exits*)

MELON: (*Claps his hands, surveys the office triumphantly, suddenly remembers his audience, turns, stares out waggishly*) Oh, what a brute! Oh, what a beast! Oh, what a brute and a beast to ride roughshod over that dear old fuddy-duddy, that's what you're thinking, aren't you, ladies? That poor, sweet, deaf old gentleman! And it does you credit, yes, your outrage does credit to your sex. To your fair, tender and gentle sex. And I stand admonished, ashamed. (*Hangs his head*) But – and yes, there's a but! Funny how there's always a but, isn't there? Whether you want to kiss it or kick it, the but's always there! (*Laughs*) Excuse my little play on words – turning the conjunction but into the part of the body *butt*, which, of course, is an Americanism for – for – I think it's the Americans who are always – um – kissing or um – kicking their – their – (*Floundering*) But, but – um – the truth is I can't – I can't quite – (*Looks at his card in panic, then remembers*) Oh, yes! That's it! The truth! The truth about Edward Ewart Gladstone. Yes, you were quite right, ladies, quite right in thinking of him as an old bore and an old nuisance, that's how I've always thought of him myself, but where you're wrong – absolutely wrong! – is in thinking that he's also an old fool. He may not have heard a word I said, but he knew he was getting exactly what he wanted. (*Taps himself on the chest*) Somebody who knew not only whom to fire, which was virtually everybody, but how – which was quickly, from top to bottom I went: senior editors, (*Makes firing noise*) editors, (*Makes firing noise*) assistant editors, (*Makes firing noise*) junior editors, (*Makes firing noise*) right down to the last clucking, maternal antique of a secretary. (*Makes two firing noises*) And then I started again, at the very bottom, driven by my vision of zestful, vigorous, pragmatic, go-ahead young athlete of a – a –

(*Lights up on* SAMANTHA. *She is pretty, bent athletically over typewriter.* MELON *blinks at her, getting her into focus, then strides over.*)

Right, Miss Eggerley, let's see what you can do.

(MELON *holds out his hand.* SAMANTHA *takes sheet of paper out of typewriter, puts it with some others and hands the sheets to him.* MELON *runs his eyes over the sheets quickly. Looks up.*)

Fair enough. Typing and shorthand both up to snuff. (*Goes to desk, sits down.*) Well, now, you say you want to be in publishing, do you, Miss Eggerley, why?

SAMANTHA: Well – I've always been interested in books.

MELON: (*Allows a long pause*) Books?

SAMANTHA: Well – literature. English literature.

(MELON *allows a long silence.*)

I'm working for my O levels now. (*After another pause*) I left school early, you see. And then I decided to go back. (*Pause*) In the evenings.

MELON: (*Quickly, accusingly*) You're planning to go to university.

SAMANTHA: (*Quickly, defensively*) Oh, no.

MELON: Not ambitious then?

SAMANTHA: Well – yes. But I like reading, you see. (*Pause*) Studying helps me read. Makes me. I don't care whether I pass the exams, really.

MELON: You're ambitious. (*Smiles, genial*) You want to go to university. Until you do you'd like to knock about in publishing. But we're just something on your way to somewhere else. Which means we'd have to replace you about the time we'd got you properly trained and useful. Right?

SAMANTHA: It's not altogether like that. Really.

MELON: No. Well, I'm sorry to hear that, Miss Eggerley. Because I want everybody here to be ambitious in some way or another. As far as I'm concerned it's about the only completely necessary qualification. (*Looks at her.*)

SAMANTHA: (*After a slight pause, looks back at him*) I'd like to work here very much. I'd do my best. I really do want to be in an atmosphere of books –

MELON: So you keep saying. But now I come to think of it, publishers aren't likely to provide it. At least this publishers. What I want here is an atmosphere of success, with no time wasted on idle reading and other forms of self abuse. (*Little pause. Laughs*) That's meant to be a joke, Miss Eggerley. With a germ of truth in it, of course. If you come to work here you'd have to get used to my jokes, and learn how to respond to them. They're not very good jokes, sometimes almost impossible to identify as jokes, but I generally help people to detect them by laughing at them myself. Rather loudly. Sometimes I even slap my knee. I see that your first name is Samantha, Miss Eggerley. What do your friends call you? Sam or Sammy?

SAMANTHA: (*Smiles uncertainly*) Well, Samantha actually.

MELON: Pity, I'd have put my money on Sammy. I've always wanted to know a girl called Sammy. (*Gets up briskly*) All right, Miss Eggerley, you can go, I'll let you know in due course. Oh, one last thing. If you come to work here, I don't want any office romances or girlish gossip in the lavatories. Or flouncing about or tears or pouting because you get the occasional sharp word from me. You'll be here to do a job, and if you don't do it with charm and efficiency, you'll be out on your bum in no time, is that understood? (*Stares levelly at her.*)

SAMANTHA: (*After a moment of anger and disbelief, stares back at him*) No job's worth being spoken to like that, Mr Melon.

MELON: I think we'll get on very well. (*Smiles charmingly*) You're hired. Starting Monday.

(MELON *continues to smile charmingly after* SAMANTHA *as she recedes into darkness, then turns, still smiling charmingly.*)

Well, there you – there you – (*Gestures towards* SAMANTHA.)
But where was I – *why* was I – with Sammy – hiring her, yes,
that was it, wasn't it, ladies, hiring her at the very bottom.
And then I – I think I need a little help again, eh. (*Attempts a
laugh, takes out card*) Say sorry. No, no, we've had that – and
that – and card number three, we're up to, aren't we? 'Don't
boast.' Oh, no, that's a general note to myself – I do hope I
haven't, if I have, my apologies, ladies. No boasting from
this time forth – yes, here we are, card number three. My
genius for unexpected recruiting at higher levels too, start
with Michael, quote old publisher's axiom, made up by self:
'Those that can, write. Those that can't, edit!' (*Laughs*) Of
course, of course, (*Slapping his thigh*) that's certainly old
Michael –
(*Lights up on* MICHAEL, *suggestion of a sitting room. Drinks
table and glasses.*)
Now tell me, Michael, is it confirmed that you're pregnant?
(*Little pause, laughs*) Sorry. I mean, of course, that you're
about to have a baby, the two of you. That Melissa's
pregnant, in other words. Is it confirmed, Michael? (*Handing
him a drink*) There you are. Kate said the other night that
Melissa had phoned –

MICHAEL: Yes, it's confirmed, Mark. She's pregnant.

MELON: Congratulations.

MICHAEL: Thank you.

MELON: If that's what you want, of course.

MICHAEL: It is. Really, we'd no idea how much we'd wanted a
child until Melissa found out she was going to have one.
Odd, isn't it? After ten years of fuss over coils, caps, pills,
right back to condoms from the barber's at Cambridge,
never failing to take precautions, we still can't work out how
the fort was breached. But I suppose our unconscious need
for a child insisted on having its way.

MELON: Oh, it's probably the other way round, it's the child's
need for *you* that insists on having its way. I mean, just think
of the little buggers – the way they go at it from the second
the testicles shoot them out – millions on millions in wave on

wave. And tough and resourceful with it. It just requires *one* little bugger to make it up the tunnel and drill the target and bob's your uncle. Or Josh your son. Or whatever you're going to call him. (*Little pause*) Or her.

MICHAEL: (*Shyly*) We thought we'd call it Jocasta if it's a girl.

MELON: Jocasta?

MICHAEL: Yes. And Marcus if it's a boy.

MELON: (*After a pause*) Marcus.

MICHAEL: Not exactly after you. But somewhere behind you, Mark, with you in mind.

MELON: I'm touched. Or will be. If it's a boy. (*Laughs slightly*) Melissa going to go on teaching?

MICHAEL: No. It's going to be a difficult pregnancy, apparently.

MELON: But afterwards? Going back to teaching?

MICHAEL: Not for a few years at least, we've agreed. She wants it to have a proper childhood. So do I. In view of my own. I don't want to make the same mistake my parents made. Which was me. (*Laughs*) Which means –

MELON: How are you going to live, then?

MICHAEL: Yes. (*Little pause*) I know. I suppose I'll just have to try and get some more book reviewing. And you never know, one of my novels might find a publisher – that agent that nearly took me on – oh, by the way, did I tell you I've started on a play? It's coming along rather – really rather –

MELON: What do you intend to do about accommodation? Battle it out in that bedsitter, the three of you?

MICHAEL: (*After a slight pause*) Well, we can't really do that, of course, not three of us in the one small room, it isn't big enough for the two of us –

MELON: Harkness and Gladstone's needs an editor. Responsible mainly for poetry and fiction. We can pay ten thousand a year. I can wangle you three mornings off a week for your writing. Well, what do you say, Michael?

MICHAEL: Well, it's generous, very generous of you, Mark – you're always such a good friend, unexpectedly good, if I may – when it really counts – but I don't think – you see, I don't think – I'd have to talk it over with Melissa, of course,

but she's already worried that I'm going to abandon what she
calls my art –

MELON: I'm not asking you to join just any publishing company,
Michael, but to join Harkness and Gladstone. It has the most
distinguished poetry and fiction list in the country. Just
think of the great names.

MICHAEL: I know. I know.

MELON: Your responsibility would be to add to them. Even to
add yourself to them. We'd want first refusal on anything
you wrote – you'd have to give us that, of course, in return
for the time off we give you for writing it. Now tell me about
your play – how far have you gone with it, when can I see it?

MICHAEL: Well, I've only roughed in a few scenes as yet. But it's
essentially going to be a comedy of contemporary manners.
Infidelity, greed, political corruption. Set in a country house.
But written in heroic couplets.

MELON: Heroic couplets?

MICHAEL: Yes, heroic couplets. Oh, I know it isn't a fashionable
form at the moment, but then no form is fashionable until
somebody sets the fashion –

(*Lights down on* MICHAEL *during this sentence,* MELON *having
turned away.*)

MELON: (*Gesturing to vanishing* MICHAEL) Heroic couplets, need
I say more? I bet most of you ladies have forgotten what they
are, think they're famous twins from the age of chivalry or
something, eh, it's such a long time since I've come across
them that I'm not sure I can quote any to give you a feel, but
the first line goes tee-tum, tee-tum, tee-tum-tee-tum-tee-
tum, the last tee-tum being a word you can rhyme with
easily, and the second line goes tee-tum, tee-tum, tee-tum-
tee-tum-tee-tum, the last tee-tum rhyming with the word
you can rhyme easily with from the last line. Got it, ladies?
So what old Michael would need for a play written in heroic
couplets would be a heroic audience, eh? Actually, it would
be like being at a tennis match, except that instead of your
head going back and forth (*Does it*) it would go up and down
– tee-tum, tee-tum, tee-tum – so needless to say, ladies, I'd

as soon publish Melissa's pregnancy diary, with all medical notes attached, than Michael's play – in fact, that was one of the minor reasons for employing him, to make sure nothing of his was ever published. I look after my friends, you see, *all* my friends, not just the talentless ones. Nobody could ever accuse *me* (*Tapping himself on chest*) of wanting to stamp out the creative urge. On the contrary, I looked for potential, encouraged it – I had a feeling for it, a great feeling for it. That's why I'm a great publisher. In a nutshell!
(*Lights up on* JACOB.)
Well, Jacob, did you bring it with you?

JACOB: Bring what?

MELON: Your synopsis, of course.

JACOB: Synopsis of what?

MELON: Of your diary of your trip to Israel. What it's really like to live on a kibbutz. I hope you haven't made it sound like a summer camp, with the fear of death thrown in. What I want from you is kibbutz life as observed by a sensitive, Cambridge-educated, middle-class Jew. Don't say you didn't do it, Jake.

JACOB: Well, actually I couldn't, Mark, as I didn't stay on a kibbutz. As a matter of fact, I didn't even go to Israel.

MELON: Where have you been these last few months then?

JACOB: In the East End working in my uncle's practice. I've been desperately busy – that's why I haven't been in touch.

MELON: What the hell do you want to go down to the East End for, surely you can do better than that? Especially as you've always claimed you wanted to be a psychiatrist –

JACOB: Yes, well, you see I have an idea that a lot of mental illness could be detected much earlier. And an ordinary practice in the East End might be just the place to do it. A lot of those patients who come in demanding nose-drops are really looking for a way of talking about their nightmares, their erratic behaviour – I want the truth of other lives. Now that I've decided to live out the truth of my own life. You see, Mark – you see – (*Pause*) I'm a homosexual. And I've decided to come out of the cupboard at last.

MELON: (*After a little pause*) Now, Jake, do try to get our idioms right. We keep our skeletons in the cupboard, and our queens in the closet.

JACOB: You're not surprised then?

MELON: To tell you the truth, I've always assumed it. So has Kate.

JACOB: Really? On what grounds?

MELON: Oh, the usual. Your lisp. Your flouncing walk. Your spiteful jokes and Mickey Mouse laugh. I suppose this means you've fallen in love, then?

JACOB: I've met somebody, yes. One of my first patients. He's a waiter. We're going to live together. His name's Wong. Half Scot. Half Chinese.

MELON: Half Scot, half Chinese, and completely Wong, eh? Well, you must bring both halves around and let Kate have a look at them.

JACOB: I'd like that. Thanks, Mark. And I appreciate your robust, no-nonsense attitude – you really do have your own kind of tact, you know.

MELON: Oh, come on, Jake, the only thing I don't understand is why you've pussy-footed around your own inclinations for so long. Being homosexual has been legal for a good five years now. Not only legal, but in some quarters mandatory. Try buying a theatre ticket, for instance – that's our book!

JACOB: What?

MELON: Well, think about it, Jake. What it's like for a sensitive, Cambridge-educated Jewish queer to work with the grimy psyches and moral disorders you're bound to come across down there in the East End. That's our diary! Much better than a kibbutz!

JACOB: Oh. Well, really Mark, I couldn't do that, you know. I mean let people talk to me thinking I was their friend and confidant, and then afterwards go back and write them up –

MELON: Oh, don't write them up, Jake. Far too inaccurate. Use a concealed tape recorder. Harkness and Gladstone will transcribe them virtually free, that is, we'll deduct the cost from your advance so you won't feel badly about our paying for them and won't notice that you're paying for them yourself. A publisher's joke, Jake! A publisher's joke – (MELON *slaps him on the shoulder, laughs, turns his head, sees* RUPERT, *on whom lights have gone up. Abandons* JACOB *abruptly mid-laugh, hurries over to* RUPERT.)

Rupert, (*Rubbing his hands*) what are you drinking?

RUPERT: Oh, just a tonic water please.

MELON: Oh, come on, Rupe!

RUPERT: No, no, really. I've been getting letters saying that I'm developing jowels. And the make-up people say they can't do anything more for me. When they shade out my jowels they give me a five o'clock shadow. Like Nixon. Not good for the chap who wants to be taken seriously as an investigative reporter.

MELON: Then I'll tell you what. A very fine malt. Almost no calories. (*Pushes one into his hand*) Then if you keep your head up, chin thrust forward – (*Does it*) oh, saw you the other night, by the way. Talking to the Russian ballerina. The one that's defected. God, isn't she a stunner? Even Kate thought she was gorgeous. What happened afterwards?

RUPERT: After what?

MELON: After the interview. Did you continue your investigations? Do report.

RUPERT: To the best of my knowledge, the BBC had her driven back to the Ritz, in a taxi.

MELON: And you didn't go with her?

RUPERT: Look, Mark, I do wish you'd understand. For some reason nature made me a one-woman man, and I've had mine. Since Ruth's death I've never wanted to make love to anybody else. I'm still in love with her, you see. Physically in love.

MELON: Look, I *do* understand something of what you feel about Kate. I feel like that, up to a point, about Ruth. But –

RUPERT: The other way around, Mark.

MELON: What?

RUPERT: Ruth was my wife. Kate's yours.

MELON: Yes, yes, yes, a slip of the tongue, but what I was trying to say is that it's well known that chastity is unhealthy. And there you are, a television celebrity, meeting lots of glamorous and attractive women –

RUPERT: Mark, do you mind? I don't want to talk about it. Please. I appreciate the concern, but –

MELON: (*Holds up hand*) OK. Not a word more. After all, when you come to think of it, it's only sex, eh? (*Laughs*) Now on to what really matters. Had a chance to think it over yet? That little project I mentioned to you?

RUPERT: Yes. Yes, I have. But, really, I don't think an autobiography at my age . . . I'd never get away with it. After all, I'm only thirty-eight –

MELON: Forty, isn't it? We're exactly the same age –

RUPERT: Yes, yes, yes, you're probably right, I don't keep a close tally, you know, but whatever age I actually am, it's too young for an autobiography. Besides, they'd want details of my personal life, and since Ruth's death I haven't had one. It's been work, work, work –

MELON: With famous people. So stick to them. Leave yourself out of it except as a genial, shrewd observer and anecdotalist – you know, telling us about tantrums in the hospitality room, camera vanity – God, in one chapter you could jump from soccer players to foreign ministers – I mean, why so shy about a book? You're not shy about sitting in a chair in front of millions of people –

RUPERT: It's nothing to do with shyness. I'm not in the slightest bit shy, bloody hell! How could I be? But if I'm going to do a book, it's got to be the right one. Like some kind of tie-in on a documentary that I wouldn't just be fronting, but editing and writing.

MELON: Ah. So you *have* given it some thought?

RUPERT: Along those lines, yes. A little.

MELON: Well, it might work. We're bound to sell enough copies on your name alone – with your face on the cover, just to remind them who the name belongs to – and, yes, why not a really big, serious subject like – like (*Snaps his fingers*) death! Can't get much bigger than that, can we? We'd have to narrow it down a bit, concentrate on – on – grief! (*Snaps his fingers again*) That's it! Lots of pictures of funerals, state funerals, family funerals, the public and private faces of grief, mob hysteria, wailing, teeth-gnashing, garment-rending, or Irish wakes, jigs and drinking, and then one picture suddenly, in the middle of all this, a single face in close-up, the mouth, the eyes, full of the realization of loss – the memories – First you write the tele version, then edit the text using the stills – I'd go with that, I really would. Anyway, think about it, I've got to be off – (*Slaps* RUPERT *on the shoulder, who is staring at him in disbelief*) Be in touch. Love to Ruth, as always, eh!

(MELON *strides purposefully off, then realization of his last speech hits him. Turns, stares towards* RUPERT, *nking into darkness.*)

Hey, Rupe, I didn't mean – I didn't mean – I wasn't thinking – (*Turns back*) Well, of course, we're all of us likely, with friends – we forget – forget things about them – (*Looks towards* RUPERT *again, now gone, looks back to audience, desperately plucks out a card*) 'Tell them a little anecdote against yourself psychopath.' What! Who put? Who put? Oh – (*Peering*) A full stop after anecdote. So it must mean tell them – that's you, ladies – a little anecdote against yourself. Then full stop. Then psychopath. So a little anecdote *about* a psychopath. But what psychopath? Which of my friends that I tried to get to write a book turned out to be a psycho – (*Lights up on* GRAEME *during this.*)

(*Not seeing him*) Oh, of course! (*Smites his forehead*) Oh, of course! Hah!

(MELON *turns, drives over to* GRAEME) Ah, Graeme, there you are! Long time no see. Sorry I'm late. Got caught at the office.

GRAEME: Yes, I'm sorry I gave you such short notice, Mark. It's not easy to get away from Aberdeen at the moment, what with various family problems, and the children, of course, but I decided I had to come and talk to you face to face. You remember when I first told you I was going to become a prison education officer, I felt I had a vocation for it, and you asked me to keep an eye out for a possible book?

MELON: I think I said I'd be particularly interested in sex offenders. Particularly middle-class married ones.

GRAEME: Well, Angus Tait isn't a sex offender. But he's a hard case all right. In fact, they don't come much harder. Which is why he's so remarkable.

MELON: Keep going, Graeme.

GRAEME: Angus Tait is almost certainly a paranoid schizophrenic, in my view. All his numerous acts of violence have been directed at obvious authority figures. Teachers, policemen, social workers, needless to say, doctors, even clergymen.

MELON: Clergymen and doctors! Really. He sounds very promising, Graeme. What did he do to them?

GRAEME: Well, for one thing he – och! I'd rather not go into the details, if you don't mind.

MELON: Well, Graeme, details are of the essence. That would be the whole point of your book, wouldn't it?

GRAEME: Ah, there's a slight misunderstanding here. I'm not writing the book. He is. In fact, he's already done it. I've got it here with me, Mark. (*Smacking brief-case*) All three hundred pages, Mark.

MELON: Good God – this could be even better – no offence, Graeme, but if it's any good –

GRAEME: Any good? Why do you think I'm here? It's a work of genius, Mark. Sheer genius! Here. Let me show you! (*Takes manuscript out of brief-case*) Just take a glance – any page will give you the flavour –

MELON: (*Looks at the manuscript, in increasing bewilderment*) It – it seems to be a poem.

GRAEME: Exactly. But not just a poem, Mark. An epic poem.

MELON: But it's in an odd sort of language. Not English –

GRAEME: No, it's a kind of patois. A mixture of Glaswegian – Gorbals – but mainly he's invented it. It only takes a line or two to get familiar with it, then you're away – there's a glossary at the back. Along with a map I drew up myself – so

you can actually trace with your finger the whole saga of
Macblone's journey.

MELON: (*Shuffles through the pages at the back*) Here's the
glossary, is it?

GRAEME: Why, what don't you understand?

MELON: Well, the title, actually.

GRAEME: (*Impatiently*) No, no – as I said, just let yourself rip and
it'll all make sense. Here (*Takes manuscript from* MELON) –
here. Any section – ah, yes, a great passage. A great, great
passage. (*Begins to read*) Ya wadna wee haach, on doon a bra /
bae al yon totsle fra fern awa / Macsleek and Macblone –
(*Looks up*) Macsleek's the hero. Macblone is the lord of the
trumpets, half-god and half-darkness.

MELON: Right. (*Nods.*)

GRAEME: Macsleek and Macblone tagaether wee had / An
together thae made ta reight an tha bad / Och the mad and
tha bad / Tha bad and tha mad / (*His voice rising*) But com
awa bad / An doon head wit mad / Fra Macsleek and
Macblone –

(*Lights dim on* GRAEME, *but not completely, as he goes on
gesticulating and reading.*)

MELON: (*Stepping away, indicates* GRAEME *with a nod of his head
and a little chuckle*) His own stuff, of course. I realized that
the moment I looked at the manuscript. You see, he hoped
I'd agree to publish it because it was the work of a
psychopathic gaol-bird, and then he'd be able to say
(*Imitating* GRAEME), 'Well, I'm glad you like it, Mark, very
glad, the truth is, I wrote it myself, you see.'

(MELON *turns, looks affectionately at* GRAEME, *still
gesticulating and reading, but in the gathering darkness*.)

Oh, if you knew these authors as I do, ladies, deceitful in
their deceptions even. The stories I could tell you – and,
come to think of it, I know you ladies, too, yes, I do, (*Coyly*)
not as ladies, I mean, naturally not, but what about all those
pages on pages you've got squirrelled away in your bottom's
drawers – desk drawers, desk drawers, that is. (*Lets out a yelp
of laughter*) Oh, I'll bet there's more than just one or two of

you, more than five or six of you, possibly even more than
ten or twenty of you ladies who have a whole novel, a
romance possibly, about some rugged chaps whipping off
your bodice – no, no, I mean chap, *one* rugged chap
whipping off not *your* bodice, of course, but the bodice of
some loving and free spirited lass, eh? (*Chuckles*) Come on,
ladies, own up! Or what about that serious and moving
study, autobiographical – with a whole poetic chapter on the
trauma of your first period and so forth, eh? So forth, so
forth, so forth. (*Increasingly mechanically, puts his hand to his
head*) Ladies – ladies, did something happen to the lights?
There was a moment there when I lost your – your faces.
Your kindly, comforting – but I see you now, there you all
are, kind um – um (*Looks down at his cards*) – and comfort –
'Don't boast.' But we've had that one. Why does it keep
turning up? 'Say sorry.' 'Don't boast.' 'Say sorry' (*Lispingly*)
– why do I keep telling myself to humiliate myself? Do I
want to win your love? Can that be it? That I came all the
way down here to Chislehurst, no Chelmsford, no
Cheltenham, no – anyway, here, wherever it is – to win the
love of you ladies? Do you want my love? Why should I want
yours? Love, love, love, that's all people talk about, think
about, write about, but the fact is (*Drawing himself up*) – I
have merely come all the way down here to Chippingham to
tell you the truth about my life. And it's not a boast, for
which I therefore do not have to apologize, to say that I was –
am, am – a great publisher who never, ever missed an
opportunity, not a single opportunity, however remote and
improbable – not a single *whiff* of an opportunity did I ever
once miss –

(MELON *stands rigid, remembering one, as simultaneously lights
up on* JOSH, *eating from a carton with a spoon.*)

MELON: Ah, hello, where's Mum?

JOSH: She 'phoned. Said she had a governors' meeting. And can
we make do with something from the fridge.

MELON: Well, I can see you already have. Been in all evening?

JOSH: No, I went around to a friend for a bit.

MELON: Ah. Which one?

JOSH: Oh, just someone from school. His name's Howard.

MELON: And what did you do?

JOSH: Well, nothing really.

MELON: I've often wondered how one does that. I've never managed it myself. It must require some special skill.

JOSH: Well, Howard – well, he wants to be a writer. And he's keen keeping this diary, you see. Putting down day-to-day stuff about his mum and his new step-dad, he promotes gigs and that sort of thing and she gets jealous all the time – then there's his new step-mum when he has to spend weekends with his dad – and then there's the dog and the cat – his dad's kept the dog – he read it out to me, you see –

MELON: Good. But did you manage to squeeze in a little work on your A levels before you went to Harold's?

JOSH: Well, a little. His name's Howard.

MELON: Just because that college is expensive doesn't mean they'll get you through unaided. You have to do a bit yourself, you know.

JOSH: I know, Dad. I did some. And I'll do some later. I really enjoyed it, Howard's diary. I thought some of it was really funny. (*Spoons some yoghurt into his mouth.*)

MELON: Really? You know, that yoghurt carton must be a miracle of packaging.
(JOSH *looks at him.*)
Well, you've already spooned down yourself three times as much as it looks as if it could contain.

JOSH: Oh. It's banana flavoured.

MELON: Ah, that explains it. Now, I'd better get on with some work. When are you going to do yours, exactly?

JOSH: After I get back from Howard's. He wants me to help pick out the best passages –

MELON: You're not by any chance on drugs, are you, Josh?

JOSH: Drugs? No, why?

MELON: Well, I'm beginning to think that such a complete lack of concern about your future can only be artificially induced.

JOSH: I'm not on drugs, Dad. I never have more than three or four joints a week, and you know about those.

MELON: I believe you. I know you never lie to me. I mean, how can you? You don't use enough words to tell lies, eh? At least with me. (*Laughs*) Just a joke, Josh.

JOSH: Oh. I told Howard you were a publisher, by the way. Hope you don't mind.

MELON: Why on earth should I? I'm not ashamed of it. (*Turns to go, turns back*) You know, Josh – the brute fact is you won't get into university without two decent A levels. And then where will you be?

JOSH: Well, not in a university, I suppose.

(*Laughs, slaps knee.* MELON *stares at him.*)

That was a joke, Dad. Sorry.

MELON: A joke! A joke!

(MELON *stares at* JOSH *in fury.* JOSH *stares back, distressed by* MELON's *rage.* MELON *whips away from him.* JOSH *stays in light, goes back to furious eating, then gradually calms his eating down.*)

For a week or two I was the biggest bloody joke in London publishing. The dynamic, aggressive, never-miss-a-chance Mark Melon missing out on the bestseller of the year that – that his son, yes, his own son, had actually tried to interest him in. But remember this, ladies, remember this, you ladies, you understand, don't you, you know what it's like trying to get through to your offspring. Especially when you're a man and your offspring is a son! We're so busy trying to do our best by our hostages to fortune, so busy worrying about them, fretting for them, coaxing them, bullying, nagging them for their own good, for their *own* good, that when they do now and then break their silence, what we listen for is the slur of drugs, the whine of the ambulance, the policeman's knock on the door. True? True? Of course it's true! But still I blame myself – there, *sorry*, at last I'm saying *sorry* – *sorry* that Harold – Howard, Howard Skart and his damned diaries had nine months at the top of the bestseller list! *Sorry* when the theatre version opened in the West End! *Sorry, sorry*, by God, I was sorry

when the television series went out, everywhere I looked –
(JOSH, *during this, has taken off his shirt, is unwrapping a
package, taking out a T-shirt, putting it on.*)
– there was his face, Harold – *Howard* Skart's face, with his
ridiculous glasses, those pubescent tufts on his upper lip and
chin, and that smirk, above all that smirk – there it was, in
newspaper advertisements, on posters in the underground,
on the sides of buses, everywhere I looked!
(*Turns, just as* JOSH *is pulling T-shirt over himself, pulling it
down. On it the face as described by* MELON, *with* HAROLD
(*not Howard*) *above it, and* SKART *below it.* MELON *stares at
it. There is a pause, during which* JOSH *produces a carton of
health food, begins to tuck in.*)
What's that?

JOSH: Oh, dried prunes and bran.

MELON: No, no, not what you're eating, what you're wearing.

JOSH: Oh, it's a Skart T-shirt. Howard gave me a dozen.

MELON: Well, that's lucky, isn't it, as you seem to have got
prunes and bran all over the face on that one.

JOSH: Oh, no. (*Laughs*) Those are meant to be his spots and
blackheads.

MELON: Ah. Oh, by the way, Josh – I've been meaning to ask.
Why did you pass him on to Haylife and Forling, of all
publishers?

JOSH: Well, because you used to work for them.

MELON: And so?

JOSH: And so they're the only other publishers I'd ever heard of.
Why? Aren't they any good?

MELON: Well, they seem to be doing quite well at the moment.

JOSH: Yes, Howard says his agent says they've given him a really
good deal on his next lot. (JOSH *yawns, scratches Skart's face.*)

MELON: Good, good. Well, um, I hope you're going to buckle
down to it this evening, eh?

JOSH: Mmm? (*Stretches, expanding Skart's face.*)

MELON: To your A levels. After all, it's not *your* diary that's the
top of the bestseller list, is it? (*Turns away, attempts to bring
himself under control.*)

Oh, I know what you're thinking, ladies, you're thinking,
'Oh, I do wish he'd stop punishing himself – and us – by
going on and on about his one teeny-weeny mistake. Good
heavens, he's a famously successful publisher, let's have
some up-beat, some lift-off, let's hear about his almost
legendary feats of alchemy, how he took hold of a lump of
pure gold and transformed it in a jiffy into a lump of base
metal.' That's what you're – (*Stops, raises a hand*) No, no, a
lump of base metal and transformed it into pure gold. *That's*
alchemy. The other way around is what we do most of the
time. With our lives, eh? (*Laughs, remembers something, laugh
turns into a checked whimper*) A card, a card – (*Scrabbles
amongst them*) 'Dish out some tips.' Dish out some – but
why? What for? Who to? Surely not to – to – (*Looks out at
them*) I'm not expected to – simply because you came to listen
to me, oh, oh, I see! (*Clapping forehead*) Tips in the sense of
useful suggestions or advice, a tip on a horse, a tip on how to
get your bodice-rippers or your period-pieces published.
Well, of course, I've already taken you through all that,
haven't I? But – but –
(*Lights have gone up suddenly on* GLADYS POWERS. *She is
looking glamorous, signing copies of a book.*)
Talking successes, however reluctant – without boasting
(*Holds his arm out triumphantly towards* GLADYS POWERS) –
just think how I, Melon the Alchemist, took that lump of
dross, a mere housewife frumping away in Neasden, and
ladies I mean *frumping*! And in Neasden! I, Melon the
Alchemist, took her, converted her with a wave of my arms
and a wag of my pen into that expanding lump of pure gold,
Gladys Powers, the bestseller! Oh, wouldn't everything be
simple, ladies, if everything were as simple as that!
(GLADYS *looks across, smiles at him.* MELON *smiles
triumphantly back, makes magical gestures with his arms.*
GLADYS POWERS *is plunged into abrupt darkness.*)
(*Laughs*) But I'm sure you know as well as I do, ladies, and if
you don't, your husbands will have told you, that all the
great achievements, in publishing just as in poetry, music,

architecture, plumbing, require: 1. luck; 2. hard work; 3. dedication; 4. cunning; 5. cunning; and 6. cunning. Right up to 10., cunning.

(*Lights up on* GLADSTONE, *on hands and knees, bent over boxes of papers, crisp-bags, etc., rooting amongst them. And on* MICHAEL, *who is studying a typescript he has just picked up, realizes it isn't the one he expected it to be, begins to search with increasing exasperation through piles of scripts, his drawers, etc.*)

And by God, I needed it. Just think what I had to deal with, ladies. On my right, ladies and ladies (*As if announcing a pair of boxers, gestures to* GLADSTONE), the celebrated Old Bore and famous Old Nuisance, Edward Ewart Gladstone. And on my left, ladies and ladies, (*Gesturing to* MICHAEL) the up-and-coming, never-to-make-his-mark, young Beaten-Down-By-Life itself, Michael what's-his-name. (*Laughs*) And that's how I had to keep them, to my right and left. Because if they ever found out they were virtually one and the same person, born a generation apart – father and son, or closer still, father and grandson – if they ever found out how kindred their spirits were, it could spell the end for the reigning champion, lord of all he surveyed, the one and only mighty Mark Melon. Of course, there was nothing I could do with Old-Bore-And-Old-Nuisance. Short of heaving him out of the window. He'd got the lawyers to make sure he was there for ever. And as for young Beaten-Down-By-Life. Well, I couldn't afford to get rid of him. I'd been absolutely right about him – absolutely right! Our dud playwright, dud poet, dud essayist, dud husband and dud father was the best editor in London. Just as much an alchemist as – (*Taps his chest*) Editing the sheerest dross into fool's gold. And lots of fools roaming the bookshops bought it. Why, he could take a manuscript by – by – why, by any of you ladies even – and when he'd finished with it, it would be respectable, publishable, saleable, and above all marketable. It might even be readable. (*Looks at* MICHAEL *tenderly*) What an inspired piece of hiring. So – so – I couldn't get rid of him. And I couldn't get rid of him. So, as always, divide and rule, eh? Divide and rule. Oh, it was such – such fun!

GLADSTONE: (*Interrupting*) Mark, a word, if you please, about that young man you brought in as poetry and fiction editor.

MELON: (*Straightening his face*) If you mean Michael, Edward, he's been with us for nearly five years –

GLADSTONE: What?

MELON: He's been with us *five years*, Edward!

GLADSTONE: Really? That long! Well, it's evident he's still very raw to our ways. Naturally we all understand he wants to cut a dash, but nevertheless I have to tell you, Mark, that I find his manners at our editorial boards quite alarming. Must he really debate quite so ferociously, while remaining completely inaudible? You will please correct me on this, Mark, but the only thing of his I heard distinctly, or distinctly thought I heard this morning, was his suggestion that we should launch sex instruction manuals, you know I've always endorsed everything you've said about both economizing and entering new popular markets, but then your common sense and energy are always accompanied by an innate good taste, Mark –

MELON: I hope and believe that that's not true, Edward.

GLADSTONE: Not at all. You deserve every tribute. But it's quite clear that that young man has yet to come to terms with what our house has always represented, and I am dismayed, yes, I admit, dismayed that it should even pass through his mind that we should give our imprimatur to such a project.

MELON: It's just that he passionately believes we should think less about literature, more about the needs of every-day folk.

GLADSTONE: What?

MELON: Needs. Of every-day folk.

GLADSTONE: A joke! A joke you say! But surely – surely he doesn't think our monthly boards – conducted at the famous long table, the table that Ezra Pound himself helped Arnold to choose – are occasions for frivolity and obscenity.

MELON: I don't know what else they're occasions for.

GLADSTONE: Exactly. Exactly. And I'll leave you to put him in his place. On a more agreeable subject. Had supper with Agnes last night, you know. Quite delicious. Such a dab hand at tasty little snacks, smoked salmon on toasted cheese, fluffed eggs on parsley pastry – and lovely, lovely reminiscences over war-time London, the rockets screeching out of the sky, and not a word, not a word about wanting us to publish any of her new, unpublished – alas! – novels, or a complaint about letting the old ones slip gracefully out of print, but then a sudden *cri de cœur* – she's living on such a paltry little pension, you know – is there anything, any little thing we might commission from her? She'd throw in her water-colour illustrations free.

(MELON *presses switch on intercom. Intercom buzzes on* MICHAEL's *desk, as* MICHAEL, *exasperated by his fruitless search, stands baffled.*)

MELON: Michael, could you pop in for a moment? Straight away?

GLADSTONE: (*Confused*) What?

MELON: I suppose we could let her do the sex manuals. But no water-colours.

GLADSTONE: Mmmm?

MELON: (*Suddenly has an inspiration*) Why doesn't she do us a cook-book, Edward? Or even better, a snack-book!

MICHAEL: (*Appears*) Oh, hello, Edward.

(GLADSTONE *turns, sees* MICHAEL, *starts.* MICHAEL *addresses* GLADSTONE *in normal voice*) I've been meaning to ask – how are Arnold's memoirs coming along? I've been thinking – would you like me to help you sort through –

GLADSTONE: Excuse me. I'm rather busy. I'll leave you to Mark –

MICHAEL: Well, if you do need any help –

(GLADSTONE *returns angrily to his office, stands fuming for a moment, resumes snuffling about.*)

(*To* MELON) Are you absolutely sure he hears me?

MELON: Yes, yes, I've told you. Yours is one of the few voices he can pick up. That's why he hates it when you shout. People look rather angry when they shout at the deaf, you see. At least that's what he told me. That's why I always make a point of grinning when I shout at him.

MICHAEL: Well, then, perhaps he just doesn't like me. Have you noticed that he always leaves the room the moment I come in?

MELON: Yes, and I'm very grateful. He's a dear old dog, but he does rather use up valuable time.

MICHAEL: Perhaps. But he never leaves a room when other people come in, in fact they usually complain that they can't get him out. And this morning, the way he kept scowling at me during the board meeting. I can't imagine what I said.

MELON: You really mustn't get paranoid, Michael. The truth is he admires you enormously, but he finds your intellect rather formidable. You make him a bit nervous. And he wasn't scowling at you this morning. He was thinking very seriously about your proposal for sex manuals. He was just telling me he believes it could be a winner. And so do I.

MICHAEL: My – my proposal! But that was a joke. I said that if we go on doing some of the things on our present list, we'd end up putting out sex –

MELON: Really? Well, I wouldn't tell Edward that. It might make him feel a bit of a fool.

MICHAEL: But surely, Mark, *you* realized it was a joke.

MELON: To tell you the truth, Michael, I thought it was such a humdinger of an idea that I didn't care whether it came in joke form or not.

MICHAEL: But you're not seriously thinking – you're not seriously thinking that Harkness and Gladstone, of all people –

MELON: Why not? Harkness and Gladstone have an obligation to take care of ordinary folk too, Michael. And what group in our society – many of them very ordinary folk indeed – gets least attention when it comes to sexual matters? (*Stares significantly at* MICHAEL) Homosexuals, of course.

MICHAEL: Well, granted but – but – (*Gives a little laugh.*)

MELON: So, following your idea through, we won't go in for any

old sex manuals, but homosexual ones. We'd be using the
name of Harkness and Gladstone to a really important social
end. Just as you've always wanted, Michael.

MICHAEL: (*After a pause*) Well – well, I must remember to try out
a few more jokes at board meetings, eh?

MELON: Absolutely. Keep them coming. I'd like you to take
charge of it, Michael. To guarantee good taste. Start with a
prospectus. Circulate it with your name on it so that people
know we're serious. And for God's sake, make sure that
Edward gets one.

MICHAEL: Right. Right. I'll start straight away. And it'll make an
exciting change from writing all those letters of rejection.
Which reminds me. One of my rejects has gone missing. I
was sure it was on my desk yesterday evening. An absolutely
ghastly novel by a woman called Gladys something. Gladys
Powers. All about what she calls the self-bondage tendencies
of women. You can imagine the sort of thing. I read some of
it out to Melissa. It made her absolutely livid. So I was
wondering if it had come your way –

MELON: How *is* Melissa?

MICHAEL: Oh. Well, you know. Dreadfully worried about
Marcus. As I am. They're threatening to expel him from his
nursery school. He's been beating up the other children, you
see. The little girls to be precise. Just runs up to them and
boots away at them until the teachers drag him off.

MELON: I used to do the same sort of thing. But then it was
considered quite natural in our day, wasn't it? (*Looks at his
watch. In sudden alarm*) Good God, I've got an author due
any moment!

MICHAEL: Then I'd better clear off. I'll start in on the prospectus
straight away. (*Begins to leave*) Oh, and if that script turns up
– Gladys um, um –

MELON: Powers, didn't you say?

MICHAEL: Gladys Powers, yes – let me know, will you?
(MELON *gestures assent.* MICHAEL *returns to his office, settles
down to the prospectus with enthusiasm.*)

MELON: (*Sits for a moment, barely containing laughter*) See, ladies,

29

see how I turned a potentially lethal situation into an office
sport. I was so good at it that – that – I tell you I could have
handled Old-Bore-And-Old-Nuisance and young Beaten-
Down-By-Life standing on my head! Now you're saying to
yourselves, 'Oh dear, oh dear, there he goes again, another
boast – and after he'd promised us not to.' Aren't you,
ladies? But I'm not boasting, ladies. I mean exactly what I
say. I could have done it standing on my head.
(*During this* MICHAEL *has put papers into a folder, carried it
into Gladstone's office, tried to attract Gladstone's attention,
failed, puts it on Gladstone's desk. Looks at* GLADSTONE
snuffling about, goes back to his own office, resumes work.)

MELON: You don't believe me, ladies, do you? 'What, stand on
his head at his age, in his condition, after all that he's been
through recently?' That's what you're saying to yourselves,
isn't it? Well, just watch this!
(MELON *stands on his head.* GLADSTONE *gets up, sees
Michael's folder, picks it up, riffles through it in incredulous fury,
then hurries into Melon's office.*)

GLADSTONE: Mark, have you seen – have you seen what that
young man has sent me? A prospectus for a – a homosexual –
(*Sputters.*)

MELON: Come in here for a second, Michael!
(MICHAEL *advances.*)

GLADSTONE: Has he – has he completely lost his wits?
(MICHAEL *arrives.*)

MELON: Edward has just been admiring your latest piece of work,
Michael.

MICHAEL: (*Beaming*) Well – thank you, Edward!

GLADSTONE: One day, young man, one day – you'll get what you
deserve. I'll see to it.

MICHAEL: (*Grins*) Well, thank you, Edward. Of course it's only a
first draft –

GLADSTONE: And that day won't be long coming, I can promise
you, Michael. (*Raises his fist.*)

MICHAEL: (*Interpreting this gesture as a salute, raises his fist back*)
Thank you, Edward.

(GLADSTONE *stares at him in disbelief, turns, stamps off.*)

MELON: So there you are, Michael. On to the second draft. Throw in some diagrams, I think.

MICHAEL: Right, Mark, I'll do that. Diagrams. Right. (*Hurries off.*)

MELON: (*Returns to his feet, dusting his hands*) See, ladies! What did I tell you? Quite literally, on my head, so if it was a boast, you see, it wasn't an idle one. No. Get that right about me, ladies. My boasts are – are never idle! And how many of your hubbies – no, no, don't tell me, I'll probably find that they can all stand on their heads. And do the hundred-yard dash in seven seconds. And climb cliff faces using clothes pegs and a frayed washing line. And swallow golf balls. And light fires by rubbing pieces of wood together with their toes while their hands are busy with a bow and arrow – oh, I know what you girls are like when you get into one sort of mood – *and* I know what you're like when you get into another sort of mood, eh? Why, even my Kate, my wife Kate – (*Stops, stares out, looks down at cards*) On to the next. On to the next. 'Modes of distribution. Transport cost efficiency. Illustrate comparative percentages, Swanage, Huddersfield. Keep lively.' Now, ladies, if you consider the location of our two warehouses when I arrived at Harkness and Gladstone, the one in Swanage and the one in Huddersfield, and then consider them in their relationship to our major market, which was, of course, London, soon to include New York, Boston, Sydney, Melbourne, Toronto, Montreal, and so forth, so forth, so forth – (*Stops, blinks*) You'll understand – understand why I – I – I insisted. To. The. Powers. That. Be. Powers. That. Be. In accounts, that is. Why – why – I – (*Lights up on* GLADYS POWERS. *Now extremely unglamorous. Frumpish in fact.*)

(*Goes over, offers his hand*) Miss Powers! Thank you so much for coming to see me. (*They shake hands.*)

GLADYS: No, no, thank you for – for –

MELON: Please sit down. (*Guides her to chair.*)

GLADYS: Thank you. (*Sits awkwardly.*)

MELON: (*After a slight pause*) Look, let's pass on the preliminary courtesies, shall we, Miss Powers? Let's get straight to the point. As we both know what it is I've asked you here to talk about. (*Opens drawer, takes out thick typescript*) *The Madonna in Chains*. Interesting title. Combines the religious with the – (*Gestures*.)

GLADYS: I've made up a list of six or seven others – 'Phyllis Unleashed' is one, and 'Uncuff me, Sir!' – that's with an exclamation mark – and 'Gladys in' – I mean, 'Phyllis in Bondage', and several more, most of them with her name in, perhaps it's better to have the heroine's name in the title. Or even just call it *Phyllis*, straight out.

MELON: *Phyllis Straight Out?*

GLADYS: No, come straight out with it, and call it Phyllis, as she's what my novel's about, after all.

MELON: Ah, yes. Old Phyllis. Look, Miss Powers – can I call you Gladys?

GLADYS: Yes. Yes, please do. Yes.

MELON: I'm Mark.

GLADYS: Mark. Yes. (*Nods, stares at him intently.*)

MELON: Well, Gladys, we're about to have a complicated little conversation. A little – rough at times, probably. After all, there you are, Gladys, the fond parent anxiously protecting her beloved offspring. And here am I, Mark, a commercial publisher on the look-out for a publishable book.

GLADYS: Yes. Go on.

MELON: Our two positions don't necessarily coincide.

GLADYS: Of course not. Go on, Mark. Please.

MELON: We won't get anywhere unless we're absolutely honest with each other. Unless we know what each other wants.

GLADYS: I agree. Go on, Mark.

MELON: Who else has seen *The Madonna in Chains*?

GLADYS: Apart from my husband, you mean? Well, almost every publisher I could find out about.

MELON: What did they say?

GLADYS: The ones who bothered to say anything said it's terrible. The dialogue's feeble, there isn't a proper plot, and

I have an eye for the sort of detail that doesn't count.

MELON: And what do you think?

GLADYS: I think I have an important talent.

MELON: So do I, Gladys.

(*They look at each other.*)

GLADYS: Go on, Mark. Please.

MELON: We've had an amazing stroke of luck, Gladys, you and I. Yesterday afternoon I popped into our fiction editor's office to have a few words about something. He wasn't there. But this was. On top of a pile of unsolicited typescripts he was in the process of rejecting. I picked it up and opened it in the middle. At the right page, it turned out. I couldn't stop reading. In fact, I took it home with me. And read out large chunks of it aloud to my wife. Kate actually clapped at some of it. Whilst I was – aroused, I think is the word. I've never come across anything quite like it before. Simultaneously erotic and angry. A kind of – respectable pornography. Of course when I went back and read the beginning, and then forward and read the end, I realized that our fiction editor was right. It's hopeless as a novel.

GLADYS: Go on, Mark.

MELON: But if we stuck to the middle section. From where you write as yourself about what a woman experiences when she lusts for a man, what happens to you physically, what happens in your imagination – your sense of humiliation, Phyllis.

GLADYS: Gladys, don't you mean, Mark?

MELON: Yes, of course. Gladys I mean, Phyllis. I mean Gladys, I mean Gladys. (*Laughing.*)

GLADYS: (*Also laughs*) I wrote that whole bit when I'd had too much sherry. The rest of it, I thought about.

MELON: Then give up thinking, and stick to the sherry. I'll do it in hardback and paperback simultaneously. We'll keep agents out of it, and deal with each other direct. When you know more about these things, you'll know that's a very good deal, Phyllis.

GLADYS: I'll have to talk it over with my husband first, Mark. Is that all right? It's Gladys.

MELON: Gladys. (*Nods*) And what does he think of your book, your husband?

GLADYS: He says it all stinks except for the middle bit.

MELON: Does he really? What does he do?

GLADYS: He's an estate agent.

MELON: I'll bet he's a damn good one. We'll have lunch then, shall we? One day next week? You can give me your decision.

GLADYS: I'd like that, Mark. Thank you. But you probably already know my decision.

MELON: The lunch will be to celebrate it.

(*They look at each other.* MELON *holds out his hand.* GLADYS *takes it. Draws* MELON *to her. They kiss.* GLADYS *takes* MELON's *hands, puts them on her breasts. Writhes seductively.* MELON *sighs.* GLADYS *goes.* MELON *watches her lasciviously, turns trembling with excitement*) So what did I do, what did I do to relieve myself of the throbbing, almost sobbing – my lust for Gladys – my excitement at the deal I knew I was going to pull off – because I knew, yes, knew in my publisher's bones, my publisher's loins – what did I? Oh, *of course*! (*Begins to undress*) What I always did – the usual thing – the quite routine thing – whatever state I was in – (*Crosses to intercom while still undressing, buzzes*) Sammy, love. Come in and take a memo.

– what every man does – given that any man could look at a lump of dross called *Madonna in Chains* and convert it into a best-selling nugget of pure gold called *Gladys Unbound* – (SAMANTHA *enters, carrying memo pad and folder.*) Ah, poppet, there you are at last, what kept you? (*Continuing to undress.*)

SAMANTHA: In one of your excitements, are you?

MELON: Yes, yes, take a memo, poppet. Take lots of memos. No, don't take any memos. We're about to have a celebration. (*Begins to undress her*) I'm giving you a forty-five-minute tea-break.

SAMANTHA: Tea-break from what? I finish work in five minutes.

MELON: (*Continues to undress her*) Then I'm giving you a five-minute tea-break. We'll do the memos tomorrow, first thing.

SAMANTHA: Five minutes!

MELON: And forty minutes overtime. An hour if you want. I'm in the mood for whatever you like this evening, poppet.

SAMANTHA: What I'd like is for you to go through my essay on *Twelfth Night* with me.

MELON: Then I shall. We'll fit in an extra twenty minutes when we're done.

SAMANTHA: No, you can't. You've got to be at the Savoy in (*Looks at her watch*) an hour exactly.

MELON: The Savoy? Why do I have to be at the Savoy?

SAMANTHA: To meet Mr McKinley, the Canadian sales representative.

MELON: What? Oh, yes. Of course. To fire him. This is for reminding me – (*Kisses her*) God, what a treasure you are, Sammy poppet. (*Further undresses her.*)

SAMANTHA: But I've got to hand *Twelfth Night* in this evening. (*Taking it out of folder*) And I only got a B minus for the *Macbeth* we did last week.

MELON: Probably my fault. But what's the point of my getting you into university, Sammy, what will happen to me, tell me that? (*Kisses her.*)

SAMANTHA: Oh, you'll always find someone for your office pokes. (*Laughs, rumples his hair*) That new tea-girl wouldn't mind a go, for instance.

MELON: Really? How do you know?

SAMANTHA: Because the other day I heard her saying she fancied somebody absolutely rotten. And who could that be but you? (MELON *laughs, stands back, surveys* SAMANTHA, *now down to her knickers, bra, girdle, stockings, lasciviously.*) Aren't you going to take the rest off? I hate standing around looking like something from a dirty magazine.

MELON: I will in a minute, poppet, don't be in such a rush – because first we kiss poppet's lovely shoulders – (*Kisses her on shoulders*) then we kiss poppet's pretty breasts – (*Kisses them*) and then poppet's delicious navel (*Kisses it*) and then

then poppet's delicious memo pad – (*Kisses it*) but the place
we love me to kiss most is just here, this little patch here,
between the top of this (*Touching her stocking top*) and the
bottom of poppet's these (*Touching the bottom of her pants*) ah,
poppet, ah, love – (*Kisses her there*)

SAMANTHA: Oh, my Mark!

(*They kiss passionately.* MELON *lowers her to the floor,
frantically continues to undress her. Lights to black.*)

MELON: (*In ecstasy*) Oh, poppet, oh, love, oh, poppet!

SAMANTHA: Oh, Mark, Mark, my Mark!

(*During this lights up on* KATE, *spectacles on, putting papers into
brief-case. She takes off spectacles, stretches, as* MELON *appears
in front of her in underpants.*)

MELON: Hello, love. I like that dress, when did you get it?

KATE: Oh – (*Looks down at herself*) about two years ago, I think. I
decided to keep on wearing it until you noticed it.

MELON: (*Kisses her*) Then your patience has paid off. God, what a
day!

KATE: Oh, bad then, was it?

MELON: No, great! A great day, Kate, love! A bit of the usual
arsing about with Old-Bore-And-Old-Nuisance, and then
with Beaten-Down-By-Life (*Laughs*) and then on to Gladys
Powers.

KATE: Oh, the self-bonding lady, the solemn sexual fantasist.
What happened?

MELON: (*Rubbing his hands*) I nobbled her. And after I'd nobbled
her I – (*Thinks briefly, checks himself*) went on to the Savoy.
Dinner with McKinley. The Canadian rep. Sacked him. And
what about you, what sort of day did you have, my love?
(*Kisses her*) What sort of day?

KATE: You really must calm down, darling. *Calm down.* You look
as if you're going to explode.

MELON: You're right, love, you're right. Adrenalin's been
flowing ever since I lassooed Gladys, slung her over my
horse, and galloped her off to the bestseller list. (*Sings
William Tell overture.*)

KATE: (*Pats her knee*) Now sit down. Sit down. Ask me again.

MELON: (*Sits on* KATE's *knee*) Ask you what?

KATE: What sort of day I've had.

MELON: Tell me, love, what sort of day have you had?

KATE: You won't want to hear about it. Too dull.

MELON: Thank you.

KATE: Oh! Except for the inter-disciplinary committee. That got nasty. So I thought of you.

MELON: Of me. Thank you, love. Why?

KATE: The question was whether we should set up a course on Misogyny and the English Male.

MELON: And what did you decide?

KATE: Well, as I say, I thought of you. And explained to the committee that as the English male was already a misogynist, he didn't need a course.

MELON: (*Beginning to undo buttons of Kate's dress, playfully, idly*) Tell me, my love, did you put this on for him, too?

KATE: (*Stroking his hair*) Mmmm?

MELON: For your lover, love. Which of us did you wear it for?

KATE: Oh, not for you, as you've never noticed it. And not for him, because he noticed it the first time I wore it, so I could never wear it again, could I, for him?

MELON: So what do you wear for him?

KATE: What I wear for you. Until he notices. Which is almost at once.

MELON: So you have to wear a new outfit every time you see him?

KATE: That's right. That's why you and I have to work so hard. To keep me in new clothes.

MELON: (*Continues to undress her*) So he likes you to look sexy for him, does he?

KATE: Of course he does. Don't you?

MELON: (*Continuing to unbutton her clothes*) What, like you to look sexy for him?

KATE: No. For you.

MELON: But how can I tell (*Raising her up*) – that when you're looking sexy you're looking sexy for me? Perhaps you're thinking about him.

KATE: Or it could be the other way around. (*Helping him to undress her*) When I'm with him, looking sexy, I'm thinking about you. (*Yawns*) Come on, let's get to bed. I've got an examiner's meeting at nine tomorrow –

MELON: Just one more question.

KATE: Only one then.

MELON: Does he dare do all that does become a man?

KATE: Who dares do more is none. So be a man and come to bed. (MELON *laughs.* MELON, KATE, *their arms around each other, walk into darkness. A pause.*)

MELON: (*Making gentle love noises*) Oh, my love – my darling Kate –

KATE: Oh, my sweet – my darling, darling, darling – (*Sound of snores, Kate's and Melon's, mingling sweetly. The alarm goes off.* MELON *reappears from blackness, utterly bewildered. Stares at alarm clock, bangs it off.*)

MELON: I warned them I wasn't ready, said I'd get caught up and certain things would tumble out – but no, they said, go on, just a pack of old ladies in Cheltenham, Chelmsford, Chippendale, Chislehurst, wherever, so look them straight in the eye and stick to your cards, but there you are, aren't you, making your judgements, despising me, well, well, go ahead, go ahead, judge and despise, but remember – I'm telling you – no, you tell me, you – you, ladies, out there, what harm did I do, what harm did we do, however often I did it, with however many – just because I had a perfectly easy, relaxed, healthy liking – yes, that's the word, *healthy* liking. And relaxed. And good. And so forth. And so forth. And so forth. (*Spitting it at them*) What harm? I didn't. None. No harm at all. I merely let the emotions rip *and* brought into play all kinds of muscles you don't use on the tennis courts, even some – certainly one (*Laughs jeeringly*) – you don't use in swimming. Hey, where are you going? You, the plump lady there waddling towards the exit, hey there, fattie, where are you off to, back home to your dreary, faithless hubby, do you think he's different, do you think he hasn't had his poppet, *his* poppet? And you – you spindle-shanks, oh, and look, flounce, flounce, flounce, look at them – the one with

the carrier bag! See her (*Points, laughs*) – do you know what they can't bear? That my Kate and I were happy! That's what they can't bear. That on top of everything else I had a happy marriage. No – no – *you* there, how dare you push your way through like that, you bloody sit down, sit down, you old cow, do you hear me? (*Bellowing*) Just you sit down and get it into your skulls that whatever you might think, I was that rare thing, a happy man. A happy, happy, happy man. Oh, God, I was happy! (*Stares at them, then looks down at himself, takes in his undress*) But where are my trousers? Why am I undressed, where are my clothes? Oh, God, I'm sorry. I'm so sorry. Please forgive me, ladies, please forgive me. (*Begins to sob.*)
(*Lights and curtain.*)

ACT TWO

MELON *is sitting on a chair. There is a large box of Kleenex on his lap.*

MELON: (*Blows his nose emotionally with one piece, then wipes his eyes with another piece*) Thank you, thank you, the lady in the blue hat, such a charming hat, for the Kleenex. (*Little pause*) I can't tell you how much the gentleness and – and pity you showed me during our tea-break. Those of you who stayed. And had tea with me. Has moved me. Yes, deeply moved me. I only wish that those who left had stayed long enough to let me apologize personally. Especially, of course, Mrs Macdonald, who went to such trouble, and arranged those quite – quite delicious sandwiches and cakes. I would have liked to have said sorry (*Raises a hand*) – no, I promise I haven't forgotten my – my solemn undertaking not to boast or to apologize to you ever again. But Mrs Macdonald was so upset and angry – rightly angry – that I'd be grateful if you'd communicate – communicate my feelings. (*Little pause*) Perhaps you'd like to move forward and fill all those now empty chairs at the front. I shan't be shouting at you any more, shall I, as you've asked me not to and – and – to be quite frank, my voice – I think I'm having trouble making myself heard. (*Takes out Kleenex, blows his nose emotionally. Surveys them, sitting to the front*) There. That's better, isn't it? Now I feel I'm just sitting among friends. In a cosy little group. And I can talk at last intimately and naturally and – as you'd like me to talk to you. As you told me you would. No boasting. No shouting. No lying. No, no. Just the truth. (*Little pause*) But you see, ladies, please believe me, you must believe me, please, when I say . . . (*Stares towards them*) that I still don't know what the truth is. No, I don't. (*Shakes his head*) That's still my problem. That I've had the experience, you see. But as the poet, some poet, famous poet, said, had the experience but missed the meaning. (*Thinks*) No. He'd had the meaning but missed the experience. So it was – in my case it was – exactly the opposite of what some famous poet said. If he was famous. Was a poet even. Not that it matters. What matters for me, even now, is that for me experience, no meaning. Now I know – yes, I know, from what one or two of you were kind enough to whisper to me at tea-time, Miss – Miss – the lady there, and the two ladies there, and you, too, madam, that you'd become rather intrigued by – by the nature of my marriage. Wanted to hear more about it. What went on behind the bedroom door, eh? (*Chuckles slightly*) No, no, please don't be embarrassed, after all, there's no doubt that in the end my – my – what word would you like me to use, ladies? Bonking? May I try bonking to see if I can catch the – the proper note for what I did? Thank you. Well, there's no doubt that my tendency to bonk wherever whenever wherever I could played – no (*Raises a hand*), became somehow involved in what eventually befell me, and it would be satisfying, wouldn't it, you'd be satisfied, a lot of people would be satisfied, why, even I, yes, I would, ladies, would be satisfied if I felt that my – fate, I suppose it was, was the consequence of a bonk bonk here, a bonk bonk there, here a bonk, there a bonk, everywhere a bonk bonk – (*Lets out a laugh, holds up his hand*) Again – sorry. And sorry for the sorry. Perhaps the word bonk leads one into a certain onomatopoeic – which means, which means, I should just explain, a word that sounds like or enacts the action it describes, if I recall correctly, as with, say – say, yes, whipping, *whip*, whip! Whip!ing – you hear it, hear the noise through the air, don't you, ladies, eh? Well, with bonking – bonking. No, it's not really the same, is it? Not onomatopoeic at all. I mean bonk isn't like – like, doesn't enact the action. (*Little pause*) I must say, I do rather miss those little cards, even though there almost certainly wouldn't have been one that would have helped me get away from bonking and on to – on to what I was trying to explain about my – my – what went wrong with me. But the most difficult thing of all to explain, ladies, is that at the beginning I enjoyed it. I had such a good time, such a wonderful, wonderful time –

(*Lights up on* MICHAEL, *an opened package in front of him. He peers into it as if for the hundredth time, shudders in disgust.* GLADSTONE *in evidence, among his cartons.*)

They were my playmates, you see. Yes. Yes, that's what they were. My playmates. (*Rubs his hands, looks from* GLADSTONE *to* MICHAEL, *then surges over, presses intercom*) Michael, I want you!

(MICHAEL *stares at the intercom, surprised at* MELON's *tone, then stiffens his shoulders as if for confrontation. Goes over to* MELON.)

So you got that package I sent you.

MICHAEL: Yes. Yes, I got it.

MELON: You didn't acknowledge it.

MICHAEL: No. To tell you the truth, Mark, I've been wondering what to say. And – and that you should send it to my home, of all places. Melissa was with me when I opened it –

MELON: Well, she's a grown-up girl. She knows about these things.

MICHAEL: Yes, but I had to explain what they were for. And I didn't sound very convincing, standing there with a pile of pornographic homosexual magazines talking about a sex manual – I tried to stop her from seeing them properly, of course, but then Marcus went into one of his tantrums and knocked them out of my hand and there they were, spread all over the floor – she couldn't believe it! And nor could I, Mark, I really thought you must have gone around the twist.

MELON: Well, I hope you didn't let Marcus get his grubby little hands all over them. Edward went to a lot of trouble to get them for you. We both want to make damn sure you're not going to turn that manual into some namby-pamby, anaemic arrows-and-diagrams business, it's got to be full-bloody blooded. Michael, got that?

MICHAEL: No, Mark. I haven't got that. I've got to draw the line somewhere. Perhaps the time has come to draw it, eh? I can't

be associated with any book that contains that kind of picture
– obscene pictures of men doing unspeakable things to each
other –

MELON: They're having a good time, Michael. Is that what you
can't stomach?

MICHAEL: What on earth do you think – what on earth do you
think people would say about Harkness and Gladstone, the
reputation of the house –

MELON: Oh, come off it, Michael. You're always gabbling on
about the reputation of the house when we all know that
what you're really interested in is your wages. And you get
bloody good wages. And whose initiative, whose verve,
whose drive, whose imagination is responsible for your
getting them? Mine. Mine, mine, mine. I'm the boyo who's
going to make it possible for you to send your son to the kind
of school he's going to need, without me you'd have to get
him into some kind of correctional institution –

MICHAEL: (*Begins to tremble*) What did you say? What?

MELON: Just letting you know the score. And by the way,
Michael, you might as well know now, Edward and I have
decided to diversify. We've decided to go into ice-skating
shows. Restaurants. Chinese, Indian, Greek. Dry-cleaning.
We're keeping an eye on spiggots.

MICHAEL: Spiggots?

MELON: Yup.

MICHAEL: What – what are spiggots?

MELON: Up three per cent on last week, that's what spiggots are,
Michael. Otherwise who the hell cares what spiggots are.
The way Edward and I see it, we'll be able to hive off the
publishing part in a year or two.

MICHAEL: Yes. Well, don't worry, Mark. I'll resign long before
you make me redundant. Right now, in fact. (*Throws
package down on desk, turns to go.*)

MELON: (*Watches him, grinning*) Michael – Michael! I'm only
teasing. Just a little joke, that's all. The trouble is my head is
spinning with such ideas at the moment – they're leaping
about like fish – and then they're out and about before I've

had a chance to think them through. And of course you're quite right about Edward's pornography. Quite inappropriate. OK? Sorry. OK? Apologies to Melissa, and little Marcus, too, on Edward's behalf.

MICHAEL: Yes. Well, you know – are you sure you're all right? I've noticed recently that you've been looking a bit – a bit feverish.

MELON: Have I? Well, I feel fine now. You have such a calming effect on me.

MICHAEL: Well, I'm glad to hear it. (*Makes to go.*)

MELON: (*Seeing package on desk*) Oh, do you mind getting these back to Edward, he keeps asking me whether they're safe. Don't worry about saying anything, I'll make quite clear what our feelings are on the matter.

MICHAEL: It'll be a pleasure to get rid of them.

(*Goes off.* MELON *stands for a moment, as if about to explode, as* MICHAEL *hands package to* GLADSTONE *with cold dignity.*) These belong to you, Edward, I believe.

GLADSTONE: (*Confused, looking at package*) What?

MICHAEL: And as they're yours, I'd rather not have them in my office, if you don't mind.

(MICHAEL *turns, stalks out, to his desk.* GLADSTONE *opens package, stares down incredulously at magazines. Makes as if to pursue* MICHAEL, *then stops. Begins to examine magazines more closely as* MELON *erupts into a roar of laughter.* MICHAEL *lifts his head, listening, as if not quite sure he is hearing properly.* MELON *stamps about the office, as lights up on* SAMANTHA, *looking upset.*)

MELON: (*Confused*) What? (*Looks at her vacantly*) Oh, there you are, what's kept you? I'm running bloody late. (*Goes over to her, begins to unbutton her dress.*)

SAMANTHA: What are you doing?

MELON: What do you mean, what am I doing? You know perfectly well what I'm doing. What I always do.

SAMANTHA: But you've just done it. In a sort of way.

(MELON *stares at her.*)

MELON: You mean – you mean we've already –

SAMANTHA: You really don't remember?

MELON: Yes, yes, of course I do, love. (*Laughs*) It's just that I'm having to go at everything full tilt at the moment, at top speed, so that sometimes they seem to be over before I think I've begun them. (*Little pause. Laughs*) That's all, love, a little memory lapse.

SAMANTHA: A little memory lapse? But how could you – even you – either you're lying to me or there's something wrong with you and you ought to see someone. Even a doctor.

MELON: Oh, come on, Sammy, we do it so often that I probably don't even notice. Like having a cup of coffee, eh, love?

SAMANTHA: (*Beginning to cry*) This is worse.

MELON: Worse than what?

SAMANTHA: Worse than the sex.

MELON: What do you mean, what was the matter with the sex? It must have been all right or I'd have remembered it, eh?

SAMANTHA: You were horrible. Rough and cold. As if I weren't there.

MELON: Oh, women, women, bloody women! You're all the same. A bit of fun in the afternoon and you turn it into some sacred ritual – oh, for God's sake, poppet, do stop weeping and hand me that package. I've got a meeting with one of our successful authors, and we don't keep them waiting, do we love? The package. (*Makes an exclamation of irritation, picks up package from desk, looks down at it*) Now who . . .?
(*Lights up on* GLADYS POWERS.)
Oh, yes. (*Laughs as he sees her, goes over to her*) Watcha, cock? (*Gives her a kiss.*)

GLADYS: You're very bouncy. Even for you.

MELON: And you look good enough to bounce. It must be all that fame. Enjoying it?

GLADYS: It's odd how quickly it becomes routine. The first time I went on television I was sick right up to the moment –

MELON: Oh, I saw Rupert brown-nosing away at you the other night. Was he fun?

GLADYS: Actually he was very nice. Calming, and at least he'd bothered to read the book properly.

MELON: No, I meant afterwards.

GLADYS: What?

MELON: What's he like in bed?

GLADYS: Mark, what on earth's the matter with you?

MELON: Oh, come on, love, you can tell me. I mean, why all agitation, did you tell him about us, how did he take it?

GLADYS: For one thing, I did *not* go to bed with him, and for another thing, I wouldn't dream – what are you doing?

MELON: (*Who has put his hand on her thigh*) Groping you, of course. To find out whether you're still wearing stockings, or whether you've gone over to the other side. You have. Tights. Oh, Gladys!

GLADYS: Will you bloody well stop that?

MELON: Sorry, love. You usen't to mind –

GLADYS: Are you drunk? Or on pills or something?

MELON: I'm never drunk, however much I drink. You know that. And as for pills – I've never taken one in my life. All I am is – is –

GLADYS: What?

MELON: Cheerful. That's what I am. Amazingly cheerful.

GLADYS: Well, I told you I wanted to talk to you about something important. Is there any point in trying or are you going to go on being cheerful?

MELON: No, no, go ahead. What's up?

GLADYS: I've got myself an agent.

MELON: Good for you, honey. You should have insisted on one the first time round. I screwed you, you know.

GLADYS: Of course I know, Mark. I knew at the time. But nobody else would have published me. So I let it go. But not any more.

MELON: No hard feelings, then?

GLADYS: No hard feelings, Mark. But I warn you, I want the best for my new book. It's a serious work. And I want people to take it – and me – seriously. You see?

MELON: Of course I see. It's perfectly predictable. Don't worry, Gladys. I've always taken you as you deserve to be taken. And I've bought you a little present to prove it.
(*Hands her package.* GLADYS *looks at it.*)

Go on. Open it. I saw them when I was doing some window shopping and you came straight to mind.

(GLADYS *gingerly opens the package, pulls out sex-shop underpants, suspender belt, leather handcuffs, etc.*)

GLADYS: (*In disgust*) How cheap!

MELON: Not at all cheap, as a matter of fact. Those knickers are pure leather, cost forty pounds, the suspender belt was fourteen pounds and those aren't any old handcuffs, you know – look, they've got your initials on them. That cost an extra fiver.

(MELON *claps his hands, laughs, looks around eagerly, and lights up on* RUPERT, *lighting cigarette.*)

Hi, Rupey-doop-doop, let's get you outside a nice fattening drink. Add a few wattles and dewlaps to those burgeoning jowels of yours – here we are – and tell us who you've been fucking this week.

RUPERT: What?

MELON: Oh, come on, Rupey, Gladys told me all about it, said the problem was to stop you tumbling her while they were filming you talking, said you've been famous for it for years, at the BBC you're known as Rupert the Bore on screen, Rupert the Bare – spelt B-A-R-E – in the hospitality room and the girlies' dressing rooms.

RUPERT: Gladys – Gladys told you that?

MELON: Pillow talk. Can't say she was altogether flattering, Rupe. In fact she said lucky they didn't do ratings on your performance in the sack, you'd do even worse than for your programme –

RUPERT: (*Unbelieving*) What on earth – what on earth –

MELON: Oh, you're not going to give us the grieving widower crap again, Rupe – Gladys and I have already issued a press release for the gossip columns – if we keep quiet about your inadequacies it might do both your careers a bit of good, eh. Oh, by the way, she sent you this.

(MELON *hands* RUPERT *package*)

Says if you're going to exchange roles you might as well dress the part. Sorry about the initials on the handcuffs, but think of it as her brand and it'll make sense.

(MELON *roars with laughter as* RUPERT *pulls out handcuffs, girdle, pants, etc. Lights up on* JACOB.)

MELON: (*Hurries eagerly over*) Ah, Jake, as I'm never late, you must be early. What'll you drink?

JACOB: No, not for me, I really don't want one, thanks.

MELON: Yes, you bloody well do. Everybody drinks in my house. That's why I'm known as Hospitality Melon. (*Pours him a large drink*) Here you are, an extra fine malt. Well, how are things, Jake, how's your sex life? Young Donald still giving you decent service?

JACOB: What? Who's Donald?

MELON: Who was it then, works in a Turkish bath, moved into your place a few weeks ago?

JACOB: David. He works at the box office at the National Theatre. As a matter of fact we've just split up.

MELON: Really, why?

JACOB: Oh, the usual reason, I expect. Because he didn't love me.

MELON: Oh, I shouldn't worry about it. Lots more where he comes from. And once you've cleaned out the box office you can run through the ushers. And then there's backstage –

JACOB: What the hell's the matter with you, Mark?

MELON: What do you mean, I feel fine. Top notch.

JACOB: I always assumed you had some contempt for homosexuals. But this – this – (*Gestures.*)

MELON: Contempt! What contempt? You'll never hear me say a word against you. Even if you do put the part of the body I most admire into the part for which I have least respect! (*Rocks with laughter*) No, no, your problem isn't that you're a queer but that you're a Jew. However much you may want the sex, all you let yourself think about is love. And when it's not love, it's shame and retribution. Face it, Jake, your cock is still under orders from the Old Testament.

JACOB: You're very sick. And that's a professional opinion, Mark.

MELON: Professional opinion, professional opinion! Come on, Jake, you mustn't let all those years of aspirin-peddling and loony-coddling down in the East End go to your head. All

you're good for is dishing out nose-drops to people with colds while they whine on about their jobs, their lack of jobs, their illegitimate babies, their legitimate babies, their wife-battering husbands, their incompetent, sex-denying wives. You've forgotten what it's like to encounter a sane, robustly healthy, cheerful, fun-loving prankster of an Englishman –
(*Lights up on* GRAEME)

MELON: Oh, hello Graeme, what do you want?

GRAEME: What do I want? But you asked me here!

MELON: (*Stares at him*) What?

GRAEME: But don't you remember? You phoned me in Edinburgh last night. After midnight. Woke the whole household up. You said it was absolutely urgent, Mark. A matter of life and death!

MELON: (*Slaps his forehead*) Good God, yes, of course! And I was right. It is! But first here – a drink – (*Slaps one in* GRAEME's *hand*) – you're going to need it.

GRAEME: (*After a pause*) Well, Mark?

MELON: (*Slowly and solemnly takes some folded sheets out of his pocket, looks at* GRAEME, *clears his throat*) It's something I've written especially for you. In fact, I'm going to dedicate it to you. It's called *The Ballad of McTit and McTwat*. (*Singing and dancing as in a Scottish jig*) Oh, here is a tale of McTit and McTwat, T'wan small and firrum / T'other long an' fat / Nah McTit and McTwat tgathurr they / Ta whoole of a wahman / Reet doon to ta pee.
(*Begins to laugh, bucks about the stage, laughing uncontrollably, becomes aware of* JABOB, RUPERT, GRAEME, *all holding their drinks, watching him as if attempting to determine his condition.*)
What's the matter with you lot? You haven't touched a drop! Come on – come on – drink up!
(*They continue to watch him.*)
(*With sudden inspiration*) I give you a toast! A toast to my Kate! Our Kate!
(*Points, and lights up on* KATE, *sitting, exhausted, unaware of the group.*)
Well, you're not bloody well going to refuse to drink a toast to our Kate, are you?

49

(RUPERT, JACOB, GRAEME *raise their glasses in Kate's direction. She looks towards them vaguely.*)
(*Lifting his*) To our Kate! Down the hatch, lads! (*Drinks.*)
(JACOB, RUPERT, GRAEME *drink. Gasp. Cough and choke.*)
A touch of Tabasco. In this house we have it in the casseroles, the jokes, and now the drinks. To add bite. What do you think, lads?
(*Lights down on* JABOB, RUPERT, GRAEME, *turning away.*)
(*Looks around at ladies, still half-laughing*) Oh, I can see what you're thinking, ladies, you're thinking what a very silly, very naughty boy! What he needs is a good slap on the bottom, then off to bed with him, eh? (*Looks around, still smiling, stops smiling as he takes in expressions*) No, no, of course you're not. You're not thinking that at all, are you? You're thinking I must have gone bonkers, aren't you? (*Blinks.*) Bonkers? Did we decide – did we decide that I mustn't use that word any more? No, no, it was the verb we turned against, wasn't it? No more bonk*ing*. But bonk*ers* acceptable. As a word, that is. Not as a condition, of course. Bonking, the verb, out. Bonkers, the adjective, in. Odd, though, isn't it, I can't think of any other adjectives that end in *ers*. Can you? Ers – ers – bonkers – (*Snaps his fingers*) crackers. There's another one. Bonkers and crackers. Now isn't that a coincidence, because that's exactly what I was, wasn't I, two adjectives ending in *ers*, absolutely bonkers. Completely crackers. And how much further could I go than to be absolutely and completely *ers*, bonk and crack, eh, ladies? (*Laughs desperately*) And so forth. So forth and so forth and so forth and so forth and – and. Now where were we? You know, if things had been different, I'd be pulling out one of those little cards about now again, wouldn't I? Preferably the one about Swanage and London, Huddersfield and London, ratio of distance to cost-efficiency factors, and how I – I – (*Tapping himself on the chest*) I single-handedly managed – to merge our Huddersfield and Swanage depots into one depot at Watford, branching in south to London, branching out north to – to Huddersfield.

Can that be right? But what would have been the point of that? That wouldn't have been cost-effective, that would have been – would have been –
(*Lights up on* KATE, *sitting on a chair, exhausted.* MELON *looks at her, looks away*) both economically unfeasible and unviable economically, so what exactly did I do that transformed the whole transport structure – (*Looks towards* KATE *again, looks away*) that saved us three quarters of a million, put us in the black, what did I do, love (*Turning to* KATE) that turned the whole thing around, transformed us in the course of an evening from such a playful, cheerful, happy – happy – yes, above all we were happy, weren't we, love, until he suddenly popped up between us. And turned everything around. And ruined everything. What did I do? (*Stares at* KATE *pleading.*) Where did he come from? He was just a game, a fiction, a pretence, a little itch we created for ourselves to scratch when we wanted, foreplay – our little bit of foreplay. For years and years. So why suddenly did he – without explanation – how did he – get into our lives? Out of our game and into my brain. And out of my brain into our lives? What was his trick? How did he manage it, love, that's what we all need to know. So tell me, tell me, tell me. I need to know. Tell me. Tell me, love, tell me, Kate, love, who he is and why you let him, love! That's all I need to know, love, eh, love, eh?

KATE: (*Shakes her head*) You're ill. You're very ill. Everybody knows it. That's where he comes from. Out of your illness. That's who he is. Your illness.

MELON: Come on, love. Speak up, love. I need to know what you just said, love. What did you say, love?

KATE: I said – (*Voice rising. Little pause, then sinking*) I said, please stop. Please stop, please, please, please.

MELON: I'll stop as soon as I know. That'll be the end of it. Just tell me who it is, that's all.

KATE: But I can't tell you who it was if it wasn't anyone. Except you.

MELON: (*Tenderly*) No, no more lies, love. The time has passed for lies. Once we have the truth we can start again, afresh.

KATE: (*Gives a little laugh*) Afresh.

MELON: Yes. Go back to doing all the things we've always done. That's what you want, too, isn't it?

KATE: Oh, yes, please.

MELON: Good. Now tell me, your bloke – this bloke of yours is a friend of mine, isn't he? I think we can say that we've established that much, can't we? So let's try and narrow the field, eh?

KATE: Oh, God, oh, God.

MELON: (*Eagerly*) What, love?

KATE: I've got a job to do, work to do, a life to get on with. And there's Josh. We have no right to put him through this.

MELON: Don't worry, love. I shan't say a word to Josh about what you've done.

KATE: He hears you. Hears your voice –

MELON: Then that's exactly why you have to tell me, so we can stop all this and get back to normal, that's what we all want. Does his name begin with an M?

KATE: An M? Yes, with an M.

MELON: I thought so, I thought so. M as in Michael, eh?

KATE: No, M as in Mark. M as in Melon. M as in Mark Melon. Mark Melon, Mark Melon.

MELON: No, I didn't think it was Michael. He hasn't got the balls.

KATE: You must let me get some sleep, you must. I've got a class at nine –

MELON: If it's somebody at the college, then it's still somebody I know, isn't it? Now let's go through them, everybody I've met that you work with at the college.

KATE: We've been through them.

MELON: Then we'll go through them again.

KATE: We've been through them again. And again and again. I have got. To go. To bed.

MELON: Of course you have, Kate. You need your sleep. All you have to do is to give me a name. Just a name, love. His name. (*Crooningly*) That's all, love.

(*Lights up on* JOSH, *eating crunchily.* MELON *whirls on him.*)

What's that you're eating?

JOSH: Cornflakes.

MELON: I thought cornflakes were for breakfast.

    (JOSH *mumbles*.)

    What? (*Intimation of danger*) What did you say?

JOSH: I said, well, yes.

MELON: To what?

JOSH: To cornflakes being for breakfast.

MELON: But it's nearly seven o'clock. In the evening. What we
    have outside this house is twilight. Not dawn. They're
    different things. Almost opposites, in some respects. So why
    are you eating cornflakes at twilight when according to your
    own statement you take them for breakfast, which everybody
    knows follows on after the dawn. Eh? (*Little pause*) Eh?

JOSH: I've only just got up.

MELON: Why?

JOSH: Didn't get to sleep all night.

MELON: (*After a short pause*) I'm waiting.

JOSH: (*In a mutter*) Lot of noise.

MELON: Indeed? What sort of noise?

JOSH: (*Shrugs*) From your bedroom. You and Mum talking, I
    suppose.

MELON: Suppose? What do you mean, suppose? Who else would
    you expect to hear in our bedroom all night but me and
    Mum. Eh?

JOSH: Well, nobody.

MELON: (*After a pause*) Have you ever heard anybody but me
    talking with Mum in our bedroom?

JOSH: Well – only the cleaning woman.

MELON: The cleaning woman? Has it ever crossed your mind that
    she might be – lesbian?

JOSH: Who?

MELON: The cleaning woman.

JOSH: Lesbian?

MELON: Why not? Stranger things.

JOSH: Well, she's a granny, isn't she?

MELON: Nonsense. She's young and black, pretty and

enlightened. One knows the type. Active. Radical. Gay rights. Possibly a dyke. Why not?

JOSH: That was the one before last. The student. Filling in. (*Turns to go.*)

MELON: Where are you going?

JOSH: Nowhere. (*Little pause*) To get an apple.

MELON: Oh, you think that's where they come from, do you, just like the food in the fridge, the clothes on your back, the money in your pocket, a modern youth's version of it all growing on trees, eh, nowhere – appropriate, as it's even stupider and vaguely nasty and justifies taking as much as you want whenever you want it, well, grasp this, grasp this, it comes from me, ī provide it, I work to provide it, I'm a great worker, that's why I'm a great provider, I provide evening cornflakes for my son, and apples at dawn for my son, and friends for my wife and my wife for my friends, one of them anyway, so sit down – sit down! And you bloody well answer my question.

JOSH: (*After a moment*) What question?

MELON: Who is it? Who is it? Who is it, who is it, who is it? (*Puts his hands to his face, stumbles away. After a pause, smiles brightly*) Oh, I'm so glad to have shared all that with you, ladies. Because it's what you've wanted to know about, isn't it? And what I've had all that difficulty getting out in front of you. (*Lifts a finger*) Us. Because that's what's meant by sharing, isn't it? Not just for my sake. Not just for your sake. For *our* sakes. Your sake and my sake. Our sakes. So – so the worst of it is over. I don't even hunger for my little cards any more. I truly don't. (*Shakes his head*) I've virtually brought us to our destination. Which turns out not to be Cheltenham. Or Chichester. Or Huddersfield by way of Swanage and Wapping, and no 'say sorries' on the way, did you note that, ladies, no sorries and not a single boast. That I can think of. And if there was one, I'd think of it, ladies, believe me! Yes, believe me! Of course there were still a few processes to go through before I got to where I am now. Calm at last, and sure of myself at last. Back to myself at last. I mean, was it young Beaten-Down-By-Life?

(*Lights up on* MICHAEL.)

Or was it a Jewish homosexual psychiatrist?

(*Lights up on* JACOB.)

Or a Scots prison-lecturing epic poet?

(*Lights up on* GRAEME.)

Or was it Old-Bore-And-Old-Nuisance?

(*Lights up on* GLADSTONE.)

Or the youthful genius Howard and Harold Skart?

(*Lights up on* JOSH.)

Which one do you think I finally settled on, ladies? I bet you've guessed it, all of you to a man, haven't you? And you're right, of course. Old Beaten-Down-By-Life.

(*Lights up on* MICHAEL. MELON *keeps a straight face for a second*.)

No, no, ladies, just my little joke.

(*Lights down on* MICHAEL.)

We all know it's him, don't we?

(*Lights up on* RUPERT, *negligently leaning against a chair, looking famous, smoking*.)

The grieving widower. But you only know because he was the one I didn't mention, isn't that right? (*Wags his finger at them*) But he was only the one I didn't mention because he was the one I didn't think of. Until the very end. That's exactly how it happened to me, ladies. I didn't think of him until I thought of him. And the second I thought of him he was right in the middle of – (*Tapping his head*) this. Strutting about inside it. Lolling at his ease in it. Jeering at me from within the confines and comforts of it. (*Turns to* RUPERT) But until then I didn't give him a thought.

RUPERT: Your wife, of course.

MELON: What?

RUPERT: You asked me who I'd been fucking today. The answer is: your wife, of course.

MELON: Is – is that a joke, or what?

RUPERT: Must be a what, mustn't it, Markie-dark-dark. As it isn't a joke. And why not? She's everything a chap in my position could want. Cares for me. Worries about me. Talks tenderly to me. Dresses sexily for me. (*Takes out contents of paper bag. Girdle, handcuffs, etc.*) The sheerest leather, and her own initials on the handcuffs. Oh, such games we have. Better even than my poor dead Ruth, you see. Especially as she's alive. So very alive!

MELON: (*Turns to* KATE) It's him, isn't it?

KATE: Who, this time?

MELON: Rupert, of course.

KATE: Oh, yes. Rupert. I kept wondering why you never thought of him. A much more likely candidate than Michael or Jake or poor Graeme. A much more rational choice. (*Gives a little laugh*) Congratulations.

MELON: So it's Rupert.

KATE: And if I said no?

MELON: You'd be lying, Kate, my love, now I know it's Rupert, I *know* it's Rupert. Rupert is your bloke as – as I'm your husband. As surely as that.

KATE: And there's nothing surer than that. Is there?

MELON: Just say it, then. Then we'll be finished. It's all I've ever wanted. Just to know. That's all.

KATE: But you say you do know.

MELON: I still need you to say it, love. Then we can all rest. Just say it's Rupert, just say it, please.

KATE: Very well, I'll say it. It's Rupert.

MELON: Oh, thank you. (*Kisses her*) Thank you, love. Already I feel so much better. So much better.

KATE: Good. Then I'll just go and – and rest at last. Such a hard day tomorrow. Such a hard day.

MELON: One thing, love. Just one thing. How often did you do it, you and Rupert?

KATE: As often as you think, I suppose.

MELON: Well, that would be once or twice a week at least, wouldn't it?

KATE: Would it?

MELON: Oh, not more, surely, love? With your busy schedules. And with you at the college and he at the BBC, right on the other side of London – no, I'd think twice a week on average.

56

Now let's see – (*Takes calculator out of his pocket*) it's been going on – when did it start precisely?

KATE: I have no idea.

MELON: A long way back then. Right back in the mists of time, eh? Well, I would say it's eight years – eight years since you first began to talk about your bloke. So then putting it at eight years, at two times a week, (*Working on calculator*) comes to 832 times altogether.

KATE: We agreed that once I said it – you said that once I'd said it was Rupert, we'd rest.

MELON: But we are resting, love. Look at us. (*Gestures*) I just want to know whether you love him, that's all. No harm in that, surely?

KATE: I have never loved anybody but you. (*Little pause*) Is there any point in my saying that I have never slept with anybody but you?

MELON: It's too late, Kate. You can't go back now. You've already confessed.

KATE: I've confessed nothing. Nothing. (*Suddenly screaming*) There's nothing to confess! You're mad, don't you see, you're mad! (*Pulls herself together*) You need help. You must get help.

MELON: I'm not mad, love. Not any longer. I just want to get to the bottom of this. Why did you and Rupert become lovers? Was it because of my little adventures? Because I had them, you wanted them too?

KATE: Your little adventures? What do you mean?

MELON: My little flings. With secretaries and ladies here and there in publishing.

KATE: Your little flings? You mean you've been unfaithful to me? All this! And *you*'ve been unfaithful to me?

MELON: Ah, but they didn't mean anything, love. That's the difference. While you and Rupert for eight years – that's something else entirely. That's a kind of love, you see. Yours and Rupert's. Rupert's and yours.

KATE: Little flings, little adventures.

(*Begins to laugh, almost hysterically.* MELON *advances on her, as if about to hit her.*)

MELON: (*Bellowing*) It's not funny, love! Oh, it's not funny!
You've got to tell me. You've got to tell me.

KATE: Tell you what? What is there left to tell? Now we both
know everything.

MELON: Did you love him more? That's what I need to know.
Did you love him more? What sort of things did you do
together? In his bed? In our bed? Did you go to restaurants?
Hotels? In the afternoon? How many people saw you? How
many people know? Who have you told? Who has he told?
Does everybody know? Am I the only one – am I the last –
the last – am I? Am I? Just answer that one question. That's
all I ask. Do you love him more? More? Oh, God, oh, God –
(*Throws himself to the floor, begins to roll around on it, in an
agony.* KATE *watches miserably, as lights down on her.* MELON
*rolls about and about a bit, screaming and wailing, then gets up
abruptly, dusts himself off.*)
Now that's what I meant – all that business (*Taking out
cigarette, lighting it*) – when I talked about behaving like a
Hashemite widow, do you remember my mentioning that,
ladies, right at the beginning, and then we tried to work out
what a Hashemite was, and I said, well, we may not know
what he is, but we all know how his widow probably
behaves, eh? (*Makes gesture with his cigarette, indicating rolling
about*) *That*'s what I had in mind. Oh, I can't tell you – can't
tell you how much better I'm beginning to feel. My gratitude
to you, ladies, and – oh, please, please don't cry – not for
me – (*Looking intently towards one*) look, here I am. You see.
Here. Quietly and – and – would you like – like one of these?
(*Picks up Kleenex box, makes to offer it. As he does so lights up
on* RUPERT, *standing uncertainly.* MELON *whirls around.*)

RUPERT: (*Sees him*) Oh. (*Laughs uneasily*) You're smoking.

MELON: Oh, well. You know me. Always one to swing against the
tide. Taking it up at forty – what can I get you to drink,
Rupert?

RUPERT: Nothing, thanks. Nothing at all. (*He looks at* MELON.)

MELON: Is there something else I can help you with, Rupert?

RUPERT: Kate asked me to come around.

MELON: Really, what for? Oh, of course, a quick dip, eh? Well, she's upstairs, in our bedroom. So why don't you pop up – we'll resume our chat when you're finished.

RUPERT: (*After a pause, controlling himself*) She asked me to come around and assure you that she and I are not having, and have never had, an affair.

MELON: Did she indeed? Do let me get you a drink, Rupert. (*Goes off, pours him one, one for himself*) Sorry. I interrupted, Rupert. Go on. (*Hands him drink.*)

RUPERT: Thank you. (*Stubs out cigarette, takes a sip*) You're right. I need this.

MELON: Here. (*Offering him another cigarette*) You probably need one of these as well. (*Lights it for him.*)

RUPERT: Thanks, Mark.

MELON: (*Looking at his own cigarette, lighting one from it*) It's going to take me a long time to get addicted, I can see that. (RUPERT *attempts a friendly laugh.* MELON *laughs back. There is a pause.*)

RUPERT: Well, that's really it.

MELON: Really what?

RUPERT: Kate and I have never had an affair. That's it. The whole story. There isn't one, Mark. Alas!

MELON: Alas? What do you mean, alas, Rupert?

RUPERT: Nothing – only that I've always admired Kate enormously. But as you know better than anyone –

MELON: Into Ruth again, are we?

RUPERT: No. (*Shakes his head*) This is no place for her. Look, Mark, we all of us, all your friends, Kate, all of us, Jacob, especially, who knows about these things – we all think you're not at all well. We don't know how to help you, other than to say that we're all deeply attached to you . . . Mark, I'd no more betray you with Kate than I would – would – (*Gestures*) Please believe that. For Kate's sake. For Josh's sake. For all our sakes. For *your* sake above all. There's no other couple – may I say – for whom I would come out at such an hour. To make such a pronouncement.

MELON: Thank you, Rupert. (*Stares at him affectionately, then throws his drink in* RUPERT's *face, then runs at him, grabs him by the lapels, shouting*) God, how you must have loved it, all the time weeping about your dead wife while you were fucking mine! Oh, you sod, you sod, you treacherous, pious, hypocritical –

(KATE, JOSH *appear from different sides. They stare at the scene aghast, then run over to* MELON *simultaneously.*)

JOSH: Dad, Dad, don't – don't – don't!

KATE: Oh, Mark – oh, God, darling –

(*Between them they pull* MELON *away. Turn to attend to* RUPERT.)

MELON: (*As* RUPERT, JOSH, KATE *recede into darkness*) Really, ladies, I do promise you, there's not much more of this to go. A few more skirmishes, a tussle here and there – restaurants were bad places for me at this period, by the way, I always seemed to end the evening just after the main course, rolling about the floor, yelping, thus giving the impression that the fault was in the kitchens. Very unfair on the chefs – I was banned, actually, from quite a few – but what impresses me now I can say it, ladies, without fear or favour, now that I've been so honest and direct and truthful and so forth and so forth and so forth, just as I promised after tea, and so forth was – was – (*Blinks. Thinks.*)

(*Lights up on* MICHAEL, *working doggedly at his desk, editing typescript. On* GLADSTONE, *amidst cartons.*)

Oh, yes. That in spite of everything, in spite of the incessant battle against reality and unreality that I waged twenty-four hours of the day. *And* the night. I still managed to get on with. My. Duties. Never more so. (*Suddenly sees own desk,* MICHAEL, GLADSTONE. *Surges over to desk, plucks package off it, rips it feverishly open. Stares down. During this* GLADSTONE *picks something out of one of the cartons, looks at it uncomprehendingly, then smiles in delight, begins to laugh to himself.* MELON *throws pages down, boiling with disgust and fury.* GLADSTONE *approaches him, carrying piece of paper.*)

GLADSTONE: Mark, Mark, I must show you – oh – (*Catching sight of one of the pages*) what's that?

MELON: It's Agnes Merrivale's shitty little snack-book, that's
what it is.

GLADSTONE: What, is it Agnes's little project? So kind of you to
have thought it up for her, Mark. I can't tell you how
thrilled she – what's that?

MELON: It's a water-colour, what do you think it is?

GLADSTONE: It's a water-colour, isn't it? (*Peering at it*) Of what,
oh, a fish mounted on a board, is it?

MELON: It's a fucking sardine on fucking toast.

GLADSTONE: How very charming. And signed as well, I see.
But Mark, what I wanted to show you – look what I found
– just an envelope, you see, there's nothing in it. But there
on the back, look (*Shows him*) – in Arnold's handwriting,
you see? It just says, Ezra and the Duke of Sussex. That's
all. And I couldn't think – and then I remembered the
story, the story Arnold used to tell. You probably heard it.
About Ezra going to spend a week with the Duke of Sussex
and when he left, just getting into the train, he leaned out
of the window and said (*Puts on American accent*), 'You
know, it's been a wonderful week. I'd forgotten what it was
like to eat good food, relaxed company, walk in the
countryside, breathe the natural air. And, furthermore, I
just want you to know that your wife is the greatest fuck in
England.' And the train pulled out and an elderly
gentleman who was in the compartment said, 'I can't
believe, sir, that I have heard what you just said – did you
really just say, sir – did you really just say that about his
wife?' And Ezra said, (*Putting on American accent*) 'I know,
I know, she's dreadful in bed, but he's such a sweet, kind,
old chap that I wanted to be generous.' (*Chortles.*)

MELON: (*Advances on him*) Do you really think it's funny? A
man betraying his host, taking his wife, you think that's
funny – oh, you old – you old –
(*Grabs* GLADSTONE *by the lapels, shouting.*)
You corrupt, rotten, disgusting, filthy-minded evil, evil,
evil – out of the window, come on, out of the window with
you!

GLADSTONE: Stop it, stop it, oh, please, please!

(MICHAEL, *who has been listening, lifts his head, bewildered. Hurries forward.*)

MICHAEL: What are you doing, what are you doing?

(MELON *discards* GLADSTONE, *throws himself to the floor, wailing. Begins to crawl away.*)

GLADSTONE: (*Pathetically*) But all I did was tell him one of Arnold's old jokes.

(*As* MELON *crawls away,* KATE *appears.*)

KATE: Why aren't you at the office?

MELON: I – I had to come home. Old Gladstone told me a joke, you see. (*Stops.*)

KATE: (*Waits, then*) You came home because Edward told you a joke?

MELON: It was a joke about treachery. And adultery. That sort of joke. So I – I tried to throw him out of the window. And then it happened again.

KATE: You tried to thow him out of the window twice?

MELON: No. That other thing happened.

KATE: (*Nods*) You rolled around the floor. Gibbering.

MELON: (*Looks at her, bewildered*) How can this be? How can it be? That I'm not myself any more, love.

KATE: I don't know.

MELON: How was your day?

KATE: Hard. A hard day. Like all my days recently.

MELON: Oh, I'm sorry. And did you see him?

KATE: No.

MELON: Are you lying, love?

KATE: I expect so.

MELON: So you did see him?

KATE: No.

MELON: But you said you were lying.

KATE: I said I expected I was. But I was lying when I said that.

MELON: That you hadn't seen him?

KATE: I was lying when I said that I expected that I was lying. Because there isn't any truth any more. So it doesn't matter whether I saw him or didn't see him, whether I say I saw him or say I didn't see him. Your truth is that I saw him. So whatever I say is a lie. To one of us.

MELON: And did you – did you – make love?

KATE: Yes or no, which would you prefer? (*Gives an exhausted little laugh.*)

MELON: Why are you punishing me, why? Because you've stopped loving me?

KATE: I'm not punishing you. I'm coping. That's what I'm doing. Coping.

MELON: Have you stopped loving me? Please say.

KATE: I'm trying, darling. Oh, God, I'm trying to love you.

MELON: I don't want you to try. I hate the thought of you trying. I want you to come back to me and be – be – be – my loving Kate. Please.

(KATE *goes to him, puts her hand on his head.*)

What I can't stand – what I can't stand is that it's him. That Rupert of all people should have brought me to this.

KATE: He didn't bring you to this. He never had anything to do with anything.

MELON: Well, I didn't, I didn't. I'm not responsible – how can I be? I was one person a few mere days ago – a whole person, perfectly at ease with my life – and now I'm somebody else entirely – I have no control – my feelings jump and hop about my insides – my thoughts tangle into each other – and I want to kill, kill, kill – I wish I could kill – someone, anyone, to put a stop to this – I remember – I have an idea that in childhood there were tantrums – yes, that's what they're like, those tantrums that took one over – one was helpless in them – that's what they're like – how can you consider me responsible? How can you blame me for what that other person did – I'm not him any longer – you must help me. Please. (*Clutches at her leg.*)

KATE: (*Gently*) You must get up. You mustn't be down there on your hands and knees like a dog. It's not – becoming, Mark.

MELON: What am I going to do, love? Love me, please. That's all I ask. Love me. (*He is crying.*)

KATE: I will, I will, oh, I will! If only you'll help me.

MELON: Oh, yes, yes. Anything. Just tell me what it is. I'll do anything to help you.

KATE: Then see someone who can help you. And then you'd be helping me, you see.

MELON: (*Suspiciously*) Who? Who is this someone?

KATE: If you do, then I'll be able to love you again. I know I will.

MELON: I love you, I love you.

KATE: Then come with me.

MELON: I can't. I want to be with you. I have to be with you.

KATE: But I can't be with you, darling. Not until you're better.

> (KATE *holds out her hand.* MELON *cowers away.* KATE *looks at him sadly, turns, begins to walk away.* MELON *scrambles after her on his hands and knees, takes her hand.*)

Come, my darling (*Gently, as to a child*), come. And everything will be all right, you'll see.

> (*She leads* MELON *a few paces to a chair, guides him into it.*)

Everything will be all right, I promise.

> (KATE *snatches her hand away, walks quickly off.* MELON *stares after her, then turns to ladies. Pause, as he deals with rejection, loneliness, despair, etc., gazing at them vacantly. Makes to speak, stops, listens. Sound of footsteps. He stretches out on sofa.* SHRINK *appears, looks at* MELON *stretched on sofa in surprise.*)

SHRINK: Get up, Mr Melon. What do you think this is? A lay-by for lay-abouts? Up, man.

MELON: (*Gets up, awkwardly*) But last week you insisted I should lie down, relax, let myself drift –

SHRINK: Last week you didn't exist for me. Last week you were failing somewhere else with someone else. You're a bit of a gad-about when it comes to failure, Mr Melon. You like to fail all over the place.

MELON: But people say they can't do anything for me – not immediately – not for years and years even –

SHRINK: Health isn't a gift. It has to be earned. You must work to be cured, Mr Melon. I can't remember how long it took to hose down the Augean stables, but by general consent, your psyche is in a fouler state than they were. We'll do our best.

Even if you're not good enough. That's all for today. Bill's in
the post. (*Laughs*) Let's hope that the day after tomorrow the
receipt will be, eh? (*Laughs, exits.*)

(MELON *takes out cigarette, lights it.* SHRINK *re-appears, stands
watching.*)

Tell me, Mr Melon, how many do you smoke?

MELON: Three, four, I don't know.

SHRINK: But you've smoked ten while we've been talking.

MELON: What?

SHRINK: You've smoked ten. That's eleven.

MELON: (*Indifferently*) Oh.

SHRINK: So you're deluding yourself, aren't you?

MELON: What about?

SHRINK: The amount you smoke. And a gross delusion at that.
Why?

MELON: What?

SHRINK: Why lie about it? Why say you smoke three or four
when you evidently smoke – what? Fifty? Sixty?

MELON: But I mean packets. Three or four packets.

SHRINK: Did you? Or did you leave packets unsaid as a way of
deceiving me?

MELON: I don't know. Does that matter?

SHRINK: Your smoking could have something to do with the
breakdown. The damage it does to your whole organism isn't
only physical. It's total. Its effect over the years on the
nervous system – (*Gestures.*)

MELON: But I've only started smoking since the breakdown.

SHRINK: Indeed? How interesting. So the breakdown has flushed
you out as a smoker. Until then, you were a latent smoker. I
consider that to be important progress. The next step is to
get you to stop again.

MELON: But then I'll just have gone back to being a – a latent
smoker, will that really be progress?

SHRINK: No, but at least you'll be able to afford my fees.
(*Laughs, exits.*)

(MELON *gets up, makes as if to speak at length, sits down again.*
SHRINK *re-appears.*)

I've just grasped something rather interesting about your
case, Mr Melon. There are one or two classic symptoms.

MELON: Oh, thank God!

SHRINK: They're of the kind we usually associate with sibling
rivalry.

MELON: Oh. But – but I haven't got any brothers or sisters. I'm
very sorry.

SHRINK: Don't worry. Doesn't matter in the slightest. In fact
quite the contrary. Not having an actual sibling to rival
meant you had to make one up. Having made him up, you
had to assault him for not existing. Which is precisely what
you did to the friend of yours who was *not* having an affair
with your wife. His not having an affair was the treachery
of the brother who didn't exist. If he had existed, he would
have affirmed the rivalry and thus his siblingness by
actually having an affair with your wife, and would have
eventually required psychiatric help himself. As it is, you've
had to come in his place. In other words *you* are your
non-existent brother. See how it all fits together, Mr
Melon? Your cure will almost be too pat, an off-the-peg
number that happens to fit your averagely proportioned
psyche to a tee – it won't raise a single eyebrow in Vienna
or San Francisco, but you'll be able to walk the streets
again in drab comfort, and that's all we want, really, isn't
it? Your plod-plod-plodder of a psyche, not your rolling-
about-the-floor fire-cracker of a one – nine years of analysis
should do the trick. Easily. (*Exits*.)

(MELON *takes cigarette packet out of his pocket, crumples it,
throws it into wastepaper basket. Takes out a fresh packet,
opens it, takes out a cigarette, crumples it, throws it into
wastepaper basket, continues to do this as* SHRINK *enters*.)
You're feeling better.

MELON: (*Hopefully*) Am I?

SHRINK: Well, look at you, man. For one thing we've stopped
you smoking. I've never seen anyone not smoke as much
you're not smoking – you must be up to the two-hundred,
three-hundred-a-day mark. Well done!

MELON: (*Gratefully*) Thank you.
(*Nods. Suddenly howls. Begins to roll around the floor.* SHRINK *watches him with disgust until* MELON *has finished.*)

SHRINK: Mr Melon, you really must start trying to pull yourself together

MELON: I can't help it. I can't help it.

SHRINK: That's a matter of opinion. Anyway, I suppose we'd better try you out on some new drugs. If those don't work, we'll try some newer drugs. By the time we've discovered what effect those have on you, there'll be even newer drugs. (*Exits.*)
(MELON *sits.* SHRINK *re-appears.*)
Now, how do you feel?

MELON: (*Inertly*) Better. Much better.

SHRINK: Good. Now we start reducing the dosage of whatever it is you're on at the moment.

MELON: No, no – please (*Becoming agitated*) – please. You promised me –

SHRINK: Don't worry. We'll give you others to counter the effect of taking you off them. We might even try the same ones. That often works.

MELON: Thank you.

SHRINK: And we mustn't forget ECT.

MELON: ECT?

SHRINK: Electro-Convulsive Therapy.

MELON: You mean electric shocks? I thought they were a thing of the past.

SHRINK: Not of your past. A jolt in the head can be as efficacious as a kick up the arse. Sometimes more so, as it's sometimes more sensitive. The truth is, Mr Melon –

MELON: (*In hope*) Yes?

SHRINK: – the truth is, you're a nuisance. And a bore.

MELON: I'm sorry. So sorry. Ohhhh – (*Lets out a wail. Throws himself on the floor. Begins to roll about, but with less and less enthusiasm, until he is rolling almost idly. He stops. Gets to his knees. Stands passively.*)

SHRINK: There. You've turned the corner. You've started to bore yourself. Haven't you?

(MELON *nods*.)

A sure sign of returning health. I don't know who will be given credit for your recovery. You've been treated to a great variety of treatments. Many of them completely contradictory. One day we may know more about what we did to cure you, and then perhaps we shall discover more about what made you ill. And so forth. For the moment we will simply have to congratulate ourselves. And so forth.

MELON: Thank you.

SHRINK: (*Turning away, stops*) But don't you congratulate yourself, Mr Melon. We've seen enough of cases like yours to know that even when you're cured, you're not actually well. In fact you'll never be actually well again. But then you don't deserve to be, do you, after all the trouble you've given everyone. I'm sure you understand that, Mr Lemon. You're an educated man. (*Little pause, raises his hand in benediction*) Now go your way, my son, and sin no more.

MELON: What?

SHRINK: You heard me. On your bike, and no more fucking about. You've got bills to pay, before you sleep. Bills to pay – (*Exits.*)

MELON: And so forth, and so forth, and so forth. You see, ladies, how it was done! It may seem arbitrary, unthought out, a hop from one brutality to the other, to the mere layman, the yous and mes who never think of the need for experts in matters of this kind until we have a need for them – but – but – whatever your doubts, ladies, look at me, by God, look at me! Oh, I know what you're thinking! Why didn't somebody just take the begger by the scruff of the neck, shake him about a bit, paddle his bottom, tell him to pull his socks up, say your prayers, gentle Jesus meek and mild, look upon your little child, pity him his simply sitting, teach him, lord, and so forth. Forth. Forth and forth. Or administer herbal tea, let him roll around the floor for a few months – nine – nine months – nine in all! (*Raises nine fingers*) But the fact is, here I am, by ladies, God, restored. And who else do I have to thank? What does it matter how they did it, or even *whether* they did it. It was done! That was all that mattered.

(KATE *appears.* MELON *stares at her, vacantly.*)

KATE: It's time to come home.

MELON: Is it, love? (*Thinks*) Oh, good.

KATE: Come along, then.

MELON: (*Hesitantly*) Right. But – but what about us, love? Are we going to be all right?

KATE: We're going to do our best. Aren't we?

MELON: But what frightens me, love, is – whether you'll be able to forgive me. That's the question. That's what's been frightening me, love. Whether you'll be able to forgive me.

KATE: You were ill. So what is there to forgive?

(MELON *puts his hand towards her.* KATE *raises her hand. They don't quite make contact when lights up on* JOSH, *who has a carton in his hand, and a spoon halfway to his mouth, which he checks when he sees* MELON *looking at him.*)

MELON: Ah, Josh. That looks good, what is it?

JOSH: Well, um, cottage cheese. It's got carrots in it. (*Little pause*) And raisins.

MELON: Well, I hope it tastes even more delicious than it sounds, eh?

JOSH: I'm glad you're back, Dad.

MELON: Thank you.

JOSH: I'd better tell you now. I probably won't be going to university. I didn't do too well in my A levels, you see.

MELON: A levels? Oh, who cares? Look at me. Ten O levels, five A levels, first-class honours degree from Cambridge, and what did it lead to? Electric shocks in a mental institution, that's what it led to. (*Shakes his head, laughs*) No, all I want from you, Josh, all your mother and I want from you is that you should be – be – you know. Be. Old chap.

(*Goes to* JOSH, *makes to embrace, but before making contact lights up on* MICHAEL, *at Melon's desk. Lights up also on Michael's office, where* GLADSTONE *is on telephone, and on Gladstone's attic, which is empty.* MELON *goes over, uncertainly.*)

MELON: Well, here I am, Michael! Full of beans! And bounce!
(MICHAEL *raises his hand abstractedly, goes on working.*)
Oh, sorry, Michael. Sorry. Didn't mean to – to disturb.
(*There is a pause.* MICHAEL, *looks up sightlessly, then locates* MELON.)

MICHAEL: Ah, Mark. I had some idea you weren't coming in till Monday. At the top of a week.

MELON: Really? Is that what we – ? Well, can't do any harm to put the toe in the water, test the temperature. Can it?
(*Nervous little laugh.*)

MICHAEL: Still, it would have given us a chance to get your office ready for you.

MELON: Oh, well it looks – it really looks – (*Looking around.*)

MICHAEL: I mean your new office.

MELON: (*Looks towards Michael's office*) Oh. Oh, I – yes. I should have thought. That we might be exchanging offices –

MICHAEL: Well, not so much exchanging. Edward's in there. You'll be in Edward's – (*Looks towards attic.*)
(MELON *looks towards attic.* GLADSTONE *is still on the telephone.*)
As he and I both need more space. If I'm going to continue as General Managing Editor. And Edward's going to continue as fiction and poetry editor. When he retires again we'll reconsider the situation, of course.

MELON: And – and until then? What will I be doing, Michael?

MICHAEL: What Edward was doing. Sorting out Arnold's memoirs. We both feel there's a very valuable book there, and that you're just the chap to find it. As Edward doesn't have the time at the moment. (*Little pause*) I don't quite know what else there is for you here, at Harkness and Gladstone, Mark. At the moment.

MELON: No, no, that's fine. Just to be in the building – and to be doing something connected with the great tradition, helping keep it alive, it'll be a privilege, a privilege and an honour, Michael, to work on Arnold's memoirs, and so forth, so forth, how's little Rufus? Marcus, Marcus. (*Raising a finger*) Sorry.

MICHAEL: We've found him a very good all-the-year-round boarding school. In Canada. We gather that he's showing signs of settling down.

MELON: Oh, good, I'm so glad, I always said he'd turn out – and in Canada, do you remember McKinley, the sales rep I – um, um –

(SAMANTHA *appears. Sees* MELON, *starts.*)

SAMANTHA: Oh. Oh, sorry. I didn't know –

MICHAEL: That's all right, love. I didn't know either. We'll be through in a minute. I'll give you a buzz.

(SAMANTHA *makes to withdraw.*)

MELON: (*Crying out*) Sammy!

(SAMANTHA *stops, glances quickly from* MELON *to* MICHAEL.)

MELON: Um – how's the (*Thinks*) – Shakespeare going, Sammy?

SAMANTHA: (*Looks towards* MICHAEL) Um, well –

MICHAEL: Sammy and I had a little talk. She's decided to stay here and make a career in publishing.

MELON: Quite right, quite right, as you've always liked books, after all, and that's the main thing, Sammy.

SAMANTHA: Well, they're better than other forms of self-abuse, I suppose, Mr Melon. (*Retreats.*)

MELON: (*Gazes after her*). What?

MICHAEL: Quoting Macbeth, wasn't she? 'This strange and self-abuse'.

MELON: But that's not – not how I remember my Sammy – not quite as I remember her.

MICHAEL: Well, probably nobody's ever quite as one remembers them, Mark, and you've been away a long time. But the thing is, I've got really rather a lot to do – and I've got an author coming in any minute.

MELON: Oh. Oh, yes. Of course, Michael. Then I'll just –

GLADSTONE: (*Who has banged down telephone, scurries towards Michael's office*) Michael, Michael, we're really going to have to do something about Agnes Merrivale, I've just spent the most dreadful hour with her on the telephone, her little success with that blasted snack-book that the lunatic

Melon commissioned from her has gone completely to her head. (*Sees* MELON, *screams, back away.*)

MELON: It's only me, Edward! Only me!

GLADSTONE: What?

MELON: (*Shouting*) It's only me.

GLADSTONE: Don't – don't threaten me – don't you – I'll have you know – (*Stands trembling.*)

MICHAEL: (*Speaking at a normal vocal level, but moving his lips distinctly*) It's all right, Edward. Mark means you absolutely no harm. He simply forgot to grin when he shouted at you, didn't you, Mark?

MELON: Yes. Yes, that's it –

MICHAEL: Mark's much better now. And we must all be kind to him. As we agreed.

MELON: Thank you. Thank you. (*Grinning and shouting*) And I'm sorry, Edward.

GLADSTONE: What?

MELON: Sorry. (*Bellowing, grinning*) Said sorry!

GLADSTONE: What?

MELON: Sorry, sorry, sorry! (*Stops, stares out at ladies*) Sorry, ladies. Sorry.

(*Pause, as lights fade on* MICHAEL, *and* GLADSTONE.)

It could have happened to anyone. I insist upon that. Anyone. To you. Or to your husband. Or son. Or daughter. Or brother. To any of us. Faithful. Promiscuous. Tempted but faithful. Promiscuous in your hearts but faithful from feebleness. To policemen, lawyers, milkmen, coalminers. To midwives, teachers, harlots and heroines. Anyone. (*Stares out*) To Mrs Macdonald, tell her, when you see her, ladies, as she organizes the sandwiches – yes, even to her. It doesn't matter how good a life you lead. How carefully you select your diet. How often you go to church. What shrinks you pay through the nose to be led by the nose by. What therapies you devise for yourself. And so forth, forth and forth. It's there. Waiting. For you! (*Pause, looks out*) And so it is, ladies and ladies, I ask you to join me in prayer. (*In a kindly and confidential whisper*) Would you do that? All kneel, please. (*Barking out*) All kneel! Have you no respect? (*Little pause*) Thank you. (*Kneels, clasps hands in front of him*) Oh, Lord, our heavenly father, if indeed you do exist, hallowed be thy name. Let me move slowly and carefully, unlikely God, taking no offence, and giving none. No need for temptation, sweet king, for there is no joy to be gained from it, only nine months in a clinic, but help me to forgive trespasses in the hope that mine will be forgiven. (*Little pause*) I am thankful for my daily bread, and pray that neither the kingdom nor anything else, especially as powerful and glorious as a breakdown, will come in my, Mark Melon's, life-time. Please settle, oh, wife and God, that where I stand is where I actually am, that what I see is all that's truly visible, that all I hear is the usual medley of human noises – and that, above all, dearly beloved Lord, my master, master, my lord, if so be so – (*The alarm rings.* MELON *scrambles rapidly to his feet, turns off the alarms. Slight pause. Then speaks with urbanity.*) Well, there we are, ladies and gentlemen. But all good things come to an end eventually, as we all know, from the nursery on. But before we disperse to our different lives, may I ask you to 'spread the word' – as we say – to other rotary clubs. (*Looks more closely*) Women's Institutes. If any of you have a friend in Ipswich or Torquay, or Huddersfield, or Watford, even, anywhere where I might find an audience such as yourselves. I'm available most days of the week, and ask only for travelling expenses which – as I've done here in – in – um – I am prepared to waive – to be met at the station, conducted to the appropriate room, put back on the train, and so forth. And the usual kind of hospitality – again, Mrs Macdonald, who left under such unfortunate circumstances, my thanks for the sandwiches, tea and cakes. Thank you. Thank you, ladies. Thank you so very much, thank you, thank you. (*Blackout. Curtain.*)

TARTUFFE

An Adaptation

Tartuffe: An Adaptation was first performed at the Kennedy Center, Washington DC, in May 1982.

The cast included:

TARTUFFE	Brian Bedford
ORGON	Barnard Hughes
ELMIRE, Orgon's wife	Carole Shelley
CLEANTE, her brother	Fritz Weaver
MARIANE, Orgon's daughter	Christine Andreas
MME PERNELLE, his mother	Margaret Barker
DAMIS, his son	Boyd Gaines
DORINE, THE MAID	Barbara Bryne
PHILPOTE, Mme Pernelle's servant	Marlene Bryan
VALÈRE, Mariane's suitor	Jeff Hayenga

ACT ONE

ELMIRE *and* CLEANTE *are sitting talking*. DORINE *and* MARIANE
are sorting through a box of jewellery. MME PERNELLE *and*
PHILPOTE *are sitting on hard-backed chairs, each reading the Bible,*
PHILPOTE *with difficulty, lips moving. A sudden burst of laughter
from* ELMIRE, CLEANTE. MME PERNELLE *shoots them an angry
glance, goes on reading.* PHILPOTE *looks towards them, grinning.*

MARIANE: (*Meanwhile, shakes her head, laughing, at a ring that*
DORINE *has put on her finger*) Oh, Dorine, I can't, can I,
Mama? Look (*Goes to show* ELMIRE) – Dorine insists, but it's
far too big and – glittery. Don't you think, Uncle? (*Showing
it to* CLEANTE.)

DORINE: Glittery! If anything, it's too dull. At least for Miss
Mariane's complexion – these were your mother's, child. If it
becomes you, you should be pleased, not ashamed.

MARIANE: I'm not ashamed, Dorine, it's just – well, the way it
catches the light.

DORINE: Won't stop Valère looking into your eyes, I promise.
(*Laughter, in which* PHILPOTE *joins*.)

MME PERNELLE: (*To* PHILPOTE) Back! Get back to your reading!
How dare you blaspheme. (*She begins to read in a low,
emphatic voice, out loud.*)

ELMIRE: I agree with Dorine, my dear, it looks ravishing.

CLEANTE: And as Valère's already asked for your hand, he won't
spurn it, now one of its fingers is sporting a fortune.

MARIANE: Oh, Uncle –

ELMIRE: But, my dear, if it makes you feel uncomfortable – is
there something of your mother's that *you* feel she'd have
wanted you to wear? What about this? Or the pendant?

DORINE: We've been through them all, madame. And each
insists on being noticeable. I tell you, madame, this ring is
the shyest thing in the collection, and she's already –

DAMIS: (*Enters*) That's it! I've had enough! I wait all morning –
all morning for Alphonse and Mélian to come by, and when I

hear them at the door at last, and rush down – they're gone. And do you know why? Because Laurent has sent them away. Told them I wasn't at home. Told them none of us was at home! And when I ask him what the Devil – what the Devil he means by it, he says his master has forbidden visitors. Tartuffe has forbidden visitors. Tartuffe! Can you believe it! First he worms his way into our home, now he's actually running our lives. Well, that's it! It's time I had a few – words – with that – that –

MME PERNELLE: Oh, I wouldn't advise that, Damis, no, no, I think you'd do far better to control yourself. For one thing, your father left Monsieur Tartuffe in charge while he's away, and for another, Monsieur Tartuffe is quite right, as always. I don't approve of all these nonsensical comings and goings either, people dropping by as if we were a café or a hotel or – or worse; the carriages on the streets, the servants hanging about the hall, the buffoonery and noise and loutish laughter – a bedlam, that's what this place is, a bedlam. And what about the neighbours, do you ever think of them? Well, I can tell you, people are talking. Yes, talking.

DAMIS: Talking! What on earth about, Grandmother?

MME PERNELLE: About the sort of thing you get up to. All of you.

ELMIRE: But what sort of thing *do* we get up to, Mother?

MME PERNELLE: It doesn't matter what you get up to, it's what you let them *think* you get up to that they talk about. And that's what matters!

CLEANTE: Well, madame, in my experience people would talk just as much if we lived like monks and nuns. More, I expect, if even half of what's said to go on in some monastries and convents –
(MME PERNELLE *lets out a cry*.)
Exactly, madame, my point exactly. Not even our holiest brothers and sisters are immune from gossip. And yet they proceed with their – um, devotions, I trust. Don't you?
(MME PERNELLE *is clearly suspicious and makes no reply*.)

DORINE: If there's any gossip going on about us, I know who'll be at the bottom of it. Daphne, and her poodle of a husband. They're always spreading gossip about others so nobody will notice what they get up to themselves. But I could tell you a thing or two about Daphne, madame –

MME PERNELLE: I'm not interested, not the slightest bit interested in Daphne or her husband of a poodle, I assure you! I was thinking of Madame Orante. Yes, Madame Orante disapproves of your household, child (*To* ELMIRE), its frivolity and – and lack of propriety. She told me so herself. And even you will agree, I think, that Madame Orante is a very model of correct behaviour.

DORINE: Oh, she is now, yes. (*Laughing*) She certainly is now, these days. But the stories about her in her saucy prime, madame, gadding about to all the balls and soirées, people used to say she could roll her eyes at two men at once, one for each eye, that's why she's got that squint. (*Laughs*) And, of course, now all her old beaux are dead, or too crippled and ancient to crawl to her door, she sits at her window squinting down at all the young people, hating them for having the fun she'll never have again, this side of heaven. Oh, madame, Madame Orante's not good from choice, madame, but from envy, poor old prune. But I'll tell you why Tartuffe doesn't like people calling on us, especially young chaps like Alphonse and Mélian: if you ask my opinion, it's because of you, madame; (*To* ELMIRE) he's jealous, you see, he's afraid –

MME PERNELLE: Stop, stop, will nobody stop this creature! Oh, oh – the smutty, vicious talk you encourage in my son's house, child! (*To* ELMIRE) Well, I've heard enough of it. (*Turning to* DORINE) You impertinent, interfering, vulgar little chit – (*To* ELMIRE) How could you permit her to wait on my son's daughter, she would be a disgrace in a – a – (DAMIS *lets out a snort of laughter.*)

MME PERNELLE: (*Glares at him*) And as for you, my lad, you're nothing but a fop and a fool. I'm ashamed, yes *ashamed* to be your grandmother, I've told my poor son so a hundred times, you'll drive him to his grave –

MARIANE: Please, Grandma –

MME PERNELLE: – and you're no better, with your pretty little
    ways and your shy little smiles, and this is too big and that's
    too gorgeous and, oh, I couldn't wear that, no, no, no – but
    you'll end up wearing them all, looking like a – a – oh, still
    waters run rancid in your case, my dear, but you don't
    deceive me – (*Turning sorrowfully to* ELMIRE.) Oh, my child,
    my child, when my son bestowed on you the honour of
    becoming his wife he also bestowed on you the honour of
    becoming the mother of his children. But what would she
    say, the poor dear woman, if she could see from her grave the
    extravagance, the vanity of the woman who has replaced her?
    If you spent as much time on your prayers as on your dress,
    oh, how healthy your soul would be! You do realize, don't
    you, child, that an immodestly dressed wife is already an
    unfaithful wife. And you, sir (*Turning to* CLEANTE), you who
    might be expected to guide your sister in her duties to my
    son and her God, well, all I can say is that if I were you (*To*
    ELMIRE) I'd go down on my bended knees to him, madame,
    and beg you to stay away from my home, sir, with your
    cynical talk and – and blasphemous attitudes. There! No
    doubt you're very shocked – but I owed it to my heart and to
    my son and to my God to speak out! And that's why you all
    hate Monsieur Tartuffe, isn't it? Because he speaks out too.
    He not only knows you for what you are but tries to make
    you into what you should be. How wise my son was to bring
    him here. How wise he was to beg him to instruct you.
    Monsieur Tartuffe sees the paths of righteousness, as he sees
    the ways of the Devil. Heed him, heed him, and you may yet
    save yourselves from damnation, shame and scandal!

CLEANTE: (*After a little pause*) In that order, madame?
    (*Suppressed laughter, perhaps, from* DAMIS, MARIANE,
    DORINE.)

MME PERNELLE: What, oh snigger away, monsieur, snigger away
    to your doom's content. I'm leaving this house, child, the
    house of my own son. And I shan't set foot in it again until
    Monsieur Tartuffe has cleansed it into a fit place for people

to visit. As he will, in spite of you! Come along, Philpote, come along – not another *second* of contamination!

ELMIRE: Oh, Mother, please don't leave. Especially like this. I'm sorry if we've given you cause – we're all sorry – aren't we?

MME PERNELLE: (*Goes to* PHILPOTE, *who hasn't moved*) I told you to come along – (*Slaps* PHILPOTE) Gawking and gaping like an imbecile – move, move! (*Turns and goes out.* PHILPOTE *runs after her.*)

ELMIRE: At least let us see you out. (*Going after her*) We must try and persuade her –

MME PERNELLE: (*Exiting*) Oh, there's no need, I know my way to the door, and I don't need you bowing and curtsying me on to the street just so you can show off your manners and costumes.

(*Exit* DAMIS *and* MARIANE.)

CLEANTE: (*Who has been about to go out, stops, comes back*) No, on second thoughts I think I'm safer here. Well, Dorine, further evidence of the power of love, eh?

DORINE: Sir?

CLEANTE: She's evidently infatuated with him. Her Tartuffe.

DORINE: Oh, nothing like as much as her son is, sir. You should see *him* at it. He talks to Tartuffe as if he were – were one of the sacred martyrs, sir, begs for his advice on this, for his permission to do that, hands him huge sums of money as soon as he as much as hints – for *religious* purposes of course, sir – and thanks him for taking the trouble to order the rest of us about and give us lectures. And it's not just Tartuffe himself, sir, but his odious little puppy of a servant: Laurent's taken it up, too – he comes yelping into our rooms, frothing and moaning about our Lord in heaven. The other day he tore one of Miss Mariane's handkerchiefs into shreds because she left it between the pages of some holy book or other, he said we were committing a hideous sacrilege. And then he went and told Tartuffe what he'd done, and Tartuffe blessed and thanked him and went and told the master, who blessed and thanked *him*. And master gives him such doting looks, sir, as if – as if – as if he were his – his mistress, sir, he actually cuddles and caresses, and fondles and pampers him, sir – puts him at the head of the table at meals, sir, picks the daintiest pieces of meat off our plates, all our plates, including madame's, and pops them on to Tartuffe's, sits admiring him as he washes them down with pints of wine, and when he sags back into his chair, belching and burping, coos out, 'Oh, are you all right, Tartuffe, oh, God preserve you, brother, you dear old chap, oh, you poor dear man, are you sure you're all right?' It's – it's disgusting, sir, that's what it is! And to think that just a short time ago, when there were all troubles and rebellions and politics, the master was famous everywhere for his good sense and manliness and courage, the king himself said how *grateful* he was to him for his loyalty, we were all so proud of him.

DAMIS: (*Enters with* MARIANE) What a pity you missed her farewell. She drew quite a handsome crowd on the street. Some of them applauding her, the rest laughing at us –

MARIANE: Father's here!

ELMIRE: Oh. (*Hesitates*) Well, I'll wait for him upstairs. Or somewhere. (*To* CLEANTE) You'll stay and welcome him back for me, won't you, my dear?

CLEANTE: Well, as a matter of fact I was just off myself, I only looked in to see how things were –

ELMIRE: Please.

(CLEANTE *nods*. ELMIRE *exits*.)

MARIANE: I'll come with you, Mama. Oh, Uncle, would you mention Valère to him?

CLEANTE: Valère?

MARIANE: Yes, our getting married. Father's stopped talking about it and – and I'm getting a little worried, will you, Uncle?

CLEANTE: Well – (*Nods*) I'll try.

MARIANE: Thank you. (*She exits*.)

DAMIS: Yes, please sound him out. I've got a feeling that – that – Tartuffe! has turned him against Valère. Poor Mariane. And you see where that leaves me.

CLEANTE: No.

DAMIS: Well, I'm in love with Mélanie, Valère's sister. So if he stops Mariane from marrying Valère – you see –

CLEANTE: Yes.

DAMIS: Thank you, Uncle. (*He exits.*)

CLEANTE: Well, Dorine, have you any emotional attachment you'd like me to discuss with him?

DORINE: I'll show you what I mean, sir. You just listen.

ORGON: (*Enters carrying a box*) Ah, Cleante. You're here then, are you?

CLEANTE: Yes, just looked in to – to see how things were. I gather you've been in the country.

ORGON: Yes.

CLEANTE: Not too much in the way of flora and – and verdure, though, at this time of year, I shouldn't think, eh?

ORGON: What?

CLEANTE: Grass and flowers.

ORGON: Grass and flowers?

CLEANTE: Yes.

ORGON: What about them?

CLEANTE: Oh, nothing. I just meant – did you go away on business or pleasure?

ORGON: To see an old friend.

CLEANTE: Ah, pleasure then.

ORGON: Pleasure! Certainly not! Do you think I'd leave my house for pleasure, when my Lord above –

CLEANTE: You went on business then?

ORGON: Yes. To see an old friend, Argaz. He wanted me to – to do something for him. Look after a few – um – papers.

CLEANTE: Ah. Well, good to see you back.

ORGON: What's been going on?

CLEANTE: Going on?

ORGON: Yes. These last few days. While I've been away. How is – everyone? Where is – everyone?

CLEANTE: Oh, I think – around the house, you know. In fact, they've just been seeing your mother off – rather emotional occasion actually – as your mother seemed to feel she might not be back for some time. So they're probably all feeling a

– a trifle (*Laughs*) – you know how it is – low, you know.

ORGON: And, um – Tartuffe?

CLEANTE: Oh. *He*'s still here, I believe.

ORGON: Ah.

DORINE: Madame your wife had a fever the day before yesterday. And a dreadful headache.

ORGON: Ah, but he's all right, is he, Tartuffe?

DORINE: Oh, yes, sir. In the pink and the plump. She felt very sick in the evening, couldn't touch her supper. Her headache was worse –

ORGON: (*Little pause*) So poor Tartuffe was left on his own, you mean?

DORINE: No, he allowed himself to sit with her while he polished off a couple of partridges and a leg of mutton, hashed. She spent a completely sleepless night. We sat by her and tried to keep her fever down.

ORGON: So poor Tartuffe got no sleep either, then?

DORINE: By 'we' I meant your son and daughter and myself. Tartuffe went straight from his mutton hash to his bed. We persuaded her to be bled, sir, madame your wife. She began to feel better in the morning.

(ORGON *makes to speak*.)

Rallied wonderfully, too, sir. He made up for the blood your wife lost by putting away four carafes of port before breakfasting on goose liver, sausage and cheese. May I go now, sir, (*Curtseying*) and tell madame how delighted you are at her recovery?

ORGON: Yes, well, everything seems to be in order, then. (*Little pause*) But perhaps I should just go and see if I can find him – hear from him himself how he is and whether there's anything he needs –

CLEANTE: Let's consider the facts!

ORGON: Mmmm?

CLEANTE: Excuse my abruptness. There's a conversation we have to have, that I had to find a way of forcing myself into. Can we look at the facts, dear, together, calmly and with dispassion?

ORGON: Certainly. (*Little pause*) What facts?

CLEANTE: About you and your Tartuffe. As far as I understand
them, you rescued him from destitution when he was little
better – sorry, *more* – sorry, *other* – than a tramp.
Barefooted and tattered robe and – and the rest of it. You
took him – no doubt from the best of motives, they do you
honour, no doubt – into your home. Which he now appears
– after you've fed him and clothed him, and his servant, I
take it? – to run. Along with your son's and daughter's
social and emotional lives. You appear to be positively
proud that this quondam tramp, who many would be
inclinded to describe as an unscrupulous parasite, has
allowed you to put yourself at his service, in a role that you
yourself seem to see as somewhere between a religious valet
and a moral butler. (*Little pause*) I refrain from discussing
my own sister's situation, in consequence. (*Little pause*)
Those are the facts, as far as I understand them.

ORGON: From what you say it's evident – sadly evident – that
you don't know the facts at all. Oh, Cleante, my brother,
my brother-in-law but still my brother, I beg you to try and
understand. Once you know him properly – you see, he's a
man – a man – a man who – (*Gestures.*)

CLEANTE: Ah huh!

ORGON: He looks at the world and says: 'This is a cesspool.'
D'you see?

CLEANTE: Mmmm?

ORGON: A complete cesspool! That's what he's made me – made
me – (*Gestures.*)

CLEANTE: A complete cesspool?

ORGON: Exactly! Yes! Absolutely! And so leads me to a perfect
detachment. From all those bonds that drag one down.
From my children, my mother, my wife – all of you
together, come to that, I could see you all die – there!
There! (*Pointing in front of him*) At my feet, without caring
so much as a – a –
(CLEANTE *snaps his fingers.*)
Yes!

(ORGON *snaps his fingers*. CLEANTE *snaps his fingers*. ORGON *snaps his fingers*.)

CLEANTE: All of them dead! (*Snaps his fingers*.)

ORGON: Every one of them! (*Snaps his fingers*.)

CLEANTE: Every one of them! (*Snaps*.)

ORGON: All of them! (*Snaps*) Oh, if only you'd seen him as I first saw him! In church! I couldn't take my eyes off him! One moment raising his arms to heaven, just like an innocent babe, the next prostrate on the ground, kissing the very flagstones in self-anger and humility! He made me feel so – so inhibited and ashamed, offering up my own awkward shy little prayers – When I left he was waiting at the doors, with a cup of holy water. He held it out to me. I took it from him. I sipped. As I lowered the cup our eyes met. And he gazed through mine eyes straight into my heart, into the very depths of my heart. I stood there pierced. I knew – even in my ignorance I knew – that a great change had come into my life. I swooned, Cleante. Swooned from revelations. (*Little pause*) When I came back to myself he'd gone. I felt such a loss, such a trembling of loss. But by the Grace of God his servant and disciple, my friend for life, Laurent, was still at prayer.

CLEANTE: How fortunate!

ORGON: I waited for him, I quizzed him about his master, I learnt that his master was poor and hungry, a holy vagabond in the service of the Lord. So I sent his master food and I sent him gifts of clothes and money, which he brought me back from his master. 'Too much, my master says, oh, far too much for minion of the Lord. We love your love. We don't desire your compassions.' And when I refused to take them back, his master sent for me to watch him distribute my gifts to the needy, the oppressed, the (*Gestures*) – and permitted me to accompany him as he spoke and blessed all those who (Gestures) – and so to learn charity from him, and at least he consented – His will be done, His will be done! – to come into my home!

CLEANTE: Ah, um – whose will, exactly, is that?

ORGON: (*With sudden anger*) His! His!

CLEANTE: Ah!

ORGON: And now my house is his house and mine father's house, touched with divine favour! His influence is everywhere, in every nook and cranny of my life, instructing me by example. Have you heard – have you heard – about the flea?

CLEANTE: The flea? No, no, I don't think –

ORGON: He killed it. In anger. At his prayers. But, oh, Cleante, the agony of Tartuffe afterwards, the tears of Tartuffe, Tartuffe's despair. I wish you'd heard him, wished you'd seen him – foaming and weeping. He, Tartuffe. For a flea. Oh, oh, Cleante, if only I could reach into your soul, as he has reached into mine. Then you'd know, as I know.

CLEANTE: Well, I do know – something of what's happened to you, anyway. Because it happens all the time to men of a – a certain age. Look, you and I, we're more than halfway through life, we live in doubt, don't we, terror, even, of – well, you know. And we long for – for certainties. At least I do. (*Laughs*) Something to make sense of all the years we can't call back. I – well, I remain a bachelor – because it's too late for me to set forth on the main adventure – a bit of a coward, you see. While you, having bravely done it once, and then again – marriage, I mean – and what greater compliment could you pay your first beloved wife than to replace her immediately, eh?

ORGON: Replace her?

CLEANTE: Well, yes.

ORGON: With what?

CLEANTE: Well, um, a second beloved wife. My – sister, old chap.

ORGON: Oh. Oh, yes.

CLEANTE: Um – um, I've lost the – oh, oh, yes. And there, suddenly you see in front of you, not a new life, through a second marriage, but doubts, fears – (*Gestures.*)

ORGON: Ha!

CLEANTE: You've no idea what you've lived for all these years, what to go on living for. And so – and so – Tartuffe! Like a gift from heaven! And suddenly it's all quite simple, just as in childhood or at school, eh? (*Laughs*.)

(ORGON *stares at him unnervingly*.)

You know what I mean – this is good, that is bad, do this, don't do that, here heaven, there hell, etc. – and – and suddenly – no more confusion, no more terrors, eh? Your love for – for Damis, for Mariane, for my sister, previously complicated and full of bewilderment – a family being a family, eh? From what I can make out of that sort of thing (*Laughs*) –um, you know, 'How do I look after them? What do they expect from me?' is reduced to a magnificent – magnificently simple. (*Snaps his fingers*) What are *they* compared to the great truth that your Tartuffe has delivered to you?

ORGON: (*Snaps his fingers*) Exactly!

CLEANTE: I think you've missed my point – I suppose I've misjudged my – my – lost, what I mean is – look, there's no clarity like blindness, don't you see? Blindness to life and all you love – that's what Tartuffe's done to you, made you blind, d'you see?

ORGON: I see. Blind.

CLEANTE: Well, yes, in a manner of –

ORGON: (*Laughs contemptuously*) Your servant, sir. (*Bows, makes to go*.)

CLEANTE: (*Hesitates*) But – one more word, though, if you please. Just on the – the question of Mariane and her Valère. You have fixed the happy day, I suppose.

ORGON: Yes.

CLEANTE: Oh, good. When is it to be?

ORGON: Don't know.

CLEANTE: Don't know?

ORGON: Decided to postpone.

CLEANTE: Any particular reason?

ORGON: Don't know if it's particular. But it'll do for me. (*Laughs*.)

CLEANTE: But you haven't changed your mind?

ORGON: Possibly.

CLEANTE: You mean you intend to break your word?

ORGON: What word?

CLEANTE: Didn't you give your word to Valère?

ORGON: Did I?

CLEANTE: Do you intend to break it?

ORGON: Do I?

CLEANTE: Well, do you? Your daughter would like to know. And so would Valère. Her fiancé. (*Little pause*) I think they both have the right –

ORGON: Indeed?

CLEANTE: What do I say to them?

ORGON: You? Why, whatever you like.

CLEANTE: Whatever I like may not be true. What are *your* plans?

ORGON: To do the will of heaven.

CLEANTE: The will of heaven must be that you honour your word, mustn't it?

(ORGON *smiles*.)

Well, do you intend or don't you, sir, to honour your word?

ORGON: Good day to you, sir.

(CLEANTE *stands for a moment, makes an angry gesture, exits*.) Tartuffe! Tartuffe! Come down! Where are you? Where is he, why hasn't he come –

(MARIANE *appears at the door*.)

Ah – (*Peers at her*) Mariane?

(DORINE *is briefly visible. It is evident that she listens to the ensuing exchange*.)

MARIANE: Father?

ORGON: Tartuffe not with you, then?

MARIANE: No, Father.

ORGON: Ah. Where is he then?

MARIANE: I don't know, Father. I thought you called me.

ORGON: What for?

MARIANE: I don't know. (*Hesitates*) Well –

(*During this* DORINE *has closed her door. Now opens it again, so that she can see in, and listens*.)

ORGON: Mariane, my dear, you're very dear to me, very dear my – um – dear.

MARIANE: Thank you, Father.

ORGON: With your exceptionally sweet nature and – (*Gestures.*)

MARIANE: Thank you, Father.

ORGON: Now, tell me – tell me, what do you think of our guest?

MARIANE: Our guest?

ORGON: Tartuffe, child. (*Little pause*) Well, what do you think of him?

MARIANE: I – I – what do you think I should think of him, Father? I think what – what you think. Of course I do.

ORGON: Ah! A most loving reply. Well, that's settled then. You shall have him for your husband.
(MARIANE *cries out, recoiling.*)
What's the matter, child?

MARIANE: I – I must have misunderstood.

ORGON: You said you thought of Tartuffe as I think of him. And I think of him as your husband. What misunderstanding can there be?

MARIANE: But –

ORGON: In joining you to him I join him to us – to all my family, in a sacred union. As you love me, so you love him. In making him my son, you remain my daughter, daughter. If I were to give you to any other man, I would lose you. For ever. Consider that!

DORINE: (*Enters, pretending to laugh*) Oh, master –

ORGON: What do you want?

DORINE: I had to come and tell you! I've just heard the most ridiculous nonsense, some – some malicious idiot is putting it about that (*Laughs*) – Tartuffe's going to marry Miss Mariane, not that anyone would believe it, even if you went around saying it yourself, would they, sir?

ORGON: It's true.

DORINE: (*Laughing*) Oh, sir –

ORGON: I tell you, it's true!
(DORINE *laughs again.*)

ORGON: It's true, true, true! I tell you it's true. It's true!

DORINE: (*Laughing*) Oh, sir, do stop – poor Miss believes you – he's only joking, Miss –

ORGON: Are you trying to drive me mad?

DORINE: No, to drive you sane, sir!

ORGON: What? You take too many liberties in this house, girl –

DORINE: Oh, please, sir, don't be angry, I only meant – well, for one thing are you sure Monsieur Tartuffe needs a wife? With so many saintly matters to worry about, and so busy guiding people to heaven and keeping them out of hell, wouldn't a silly little wife just get in the way?

ORGON: He would soon make her serious, and a help to him. Through prayer and instruction, my child. Rejoice.

DORINE: Well, but, sir, from the business point of view, have you given that enough thought? An appetite like that in the family – just consider how much he eats and drinks, sir, and not a penny to his name, not a very practical – (*Calms down.*)

ORGON: (*Bellowing*) Now try – try to understand. His poverty is a dowry. His hatred of wordly goods raises him above the world, to far, far greater riches. Those riches he brings to you, my child. Rejoice.

DORINE: Oh. Well, in that case he won't want what she brings him, will he, sir? *Her* dowry, I mean –

ORGON: What he wants and what I want have nothing to do with you!

DORINE: What about what Miss Mariane wants, sir? And that's Monsieur Valère. (*To* MARIANE) Isn't it?

ORGON: Kindly do not try to drag my daughter into this. Although, as you've mentioned Valère – I regret to inform you, my dear, that I've unmasked a number of weaknesses in our young Valère that would make him an unsuitable husband, even if you were free, which, of course, you no longer are. For one thing he's an inveterate gambler –

DORINE: For a few shillings. At cards. With his friends –

ORGON: – and for another he's not serious. You've noticed yourself, I'm sure, his tendency to laugh and make jokes all the time. And finally and most importantly, I have grounds for believing that – he's a free thinker! I have never once seen him at church. Not once!

DORINE: Perhaps he goes at different times, in which case he

could say he'd never seen you at church either, sir, couldn't
he? Does that make you a free thinker?

ORGON: (*Confused*) What?

DORINE: I was just wondering –

ORGON: Then wonder to yourself. I am talking to my daughter.
Now, my dear, try to think of the pleasure, the joy, you'll
share with Tartuffe. I warrant you that once you're used to
him the two of you will be like, why, turtle-doves, billing
and cooing away at each other all day, all (*Checks himself*) –
and how good you'll be for each other, he with his strength
and passion – religious passion – and you – oh, I can see what
you'll be able to make of him, my dear, with your enchanting
little ways, eh? (*Chuckles.*)

DORINE: A cuckold.

ORGON: What? What did you say?

DORINE: A cuckold, sir, that's what I said. Because that's what
she'll make of him, well, it stands to reason, master – how
can you expect her to be a faithful wife when you hand her
over to a man she loathes, and even if she is, nobody will
believe it, will they, sir, everyone will take it for granted that
she'll have somebody else, quite a few somebody elses to
make up, won't they, sir, so in the end she might as well
anyway. I mean, why expect her to have the bad reputation
without the pleasure of earning it, poor lamb, and she can
always tell herself it's not her fault either way, it'll be yours,
master, for leading her directly into temptation –

ORGON: One more word – one more word out of you – and you'll
get the back of this! Understood?

DORINE: Yes, master.

(ORGON *turns back to* MARIANE.)

I was only trying to warn you, sir, so that I couldn't say 'I
told you so' afterwards, and I don't want people going
around laughing at you for marrying your daughter off to a
fraud and a bigot, that's all, sir, and it's not as if he'll be
happy either, women have ways of making life miserable for
men the –

ORGON: (*Advancing on* DORINE) I warn you! I warn you!

(DORINE *nods. They stand staring at each other.*)

Your last chance!

(DORINE *nods.*)

(*Turns back to* MARIANE) Now, my child, I hope you understand (*Glances at* DORINE) – that what I propose for you (*Glances at* DORINE) – is – is – um (*Glances at* DORINE) – and that you believe the husband I selected is (*Glances at* DORINE) – is – (*In a roar*) Well!

(DORINE *shakes her head.* ORGON *turns back to* MARIANE, *makes to speak, turns back to* DORINE, *his hand raised.*)

Go on. One word. Say one word!

(DORINE *stares at him.* ORGON *turns, looks at* MARIANE. *Opens his mouth.*)

DORINE: Never. That's the word. Never, never, never. I'd never, never, never let myself be forced into marriage with that brute –

(ORGON *rushes to her.* DORINE *skips out of the way.*)

Never, never.

(DORINE *runs out of the room.* ORGON *makes to run after her. Stops himself, stares around as if in momentary bewilderment. Then, as if seeing* MARIANE, *goes to her. Stands for a moment, as if about to speak.*)

ORGON: That – that girl has made me – I – I – I – where is he? I must go and find him. I – I – (*Turns, goes to the door. Stops. Turns*) So what it comes to is this. I've decided. You'll obey. Nothing more to be said. Nothing. (*He goes out.*)

DORINE: (*Has been watching from behind the other door, enters*) What's the matter with you? Have you lost your tongue? You should have been saying those things to him, not me.

MARIANE: I couldn't.

DORINE: Why not?

MARIANE: He's my father. I'm not brave enough to defy him. Dorine.

DORINE: I see. You don't love Valère then?

MARIANE: Of course I do. You know I do.

DORINE: Well then? What are you going to do about Tartuffe? Have you got a plan?

MARIANE: (*After a little pause*) Yes.

DORINE: What?

MARIANE: I shall kill myself.

DORINE: (*Claps her hands*) How clever! I'd never have thought of that! And it would solve all your other problems as well. Idiot!

MARIANE: Oh, Dorine – have pity –

DORINE: I'm not wasting my pity on a weakling.

MARIANE: But what can I do? Anyway, why should I have to do anything? Valère should do it – if he loves me as I love him.

DORINE: But if your father's gone mad, and fallen in love with a fraud of a bigot, and won't let you marry Valère, what *can* he do about it? Or do you think it's his fault? The only person who can do anything is you, and you know it, and what you have to do is tell your father you won't be ordered into a marriage you don't want, and you know that too. Don't you?

MARIANE: But I've told you – I can't – I don't know my father any more. And he doesn't seem to know me – or want to know me.

DORINE: You don't have to know each other particularly well to say no to him. He'll understand what it means. No. (*Little pause*) No, love, you must. You must find the courage.

MARIANE: (*After a small pause, in a low voice*) And my modesty?

DORINE: Your modesty?

MARIANE: If I – if I defy my father, everyone will know it's because of Valère.

DORINE: Yes. (*Looks at her*) Oh, I see! That's not your modesty, it's your pride. Well, of course, if you're ashamed of having people know you love the man you want to marry – then that settles it, my dear, naturally. And anyway, what's so dreadful about Tartuffe? He's a man of substance and weight, a man not to be trifled with. I wouldn't want to trifle with him, certainly not, and with those fine red ears and magnificent whiskers and those jowls, and those eyes that burn with passion when they look at pork and port and cheese – think of them turned on you!

MARIANE: Oh, God.

DORINE: And those arms around you – those lips pressing against yours – that stomach –

MARIANE: Oh, God!

DORINE: Night after night. And what a wedding it'll be! You and Tartuffe kneeling together, perhaps you can persuade him to say the prayers himself, *and* deliver the sermon, and then turning to face the congregation – how they'll admire your modesty and your pride then – as you walk arm in arm down the aisle – oh, I shouldn't think Valère will dare to show his face, presumptuous young popinjay for thinking he meant anything to you at all – and then your wedding night, the lips – the whiskers, the jowls. The eyes. The stomach – your first taste of your husband, your lord, your master. For night after night. For year on year –

MARIANE: You're killing me, Dorine!

DORINE: Your servant, mademoiselle.

MARIANE: Please – Dorine, please help me!

DORINE: To do what? It's all arranged. You're to be – Tartuffed. And Tartuffed *and* Tartuffed. Night after night. Year on year.

MARIANE: I shan't have to kill myself. I'll die anyway. (*Pause*) Oh, Dorine – (*Throws herself into* DORINE's *arms.*)

DORINE: (*Stroking her hair*) There, there, child.
There, there – we'll find a way. We'll find a way – ah, Valère. (*Curtsies*) Your servant, sir.

VALÈRE: (*As he enters*) I've just heard – I've just heard the most amusing piece of news. From one of your footmen. Who got it from Tartuffe's servant. Who, I suppose, got it from Tartuffe himself. Who, I suppose, got it from you, mademoiselle.

MARIANE: Indeed? What, monsieur?

VALÈRE: That you're going to marry him. Or is that as much of a surprise to you as it was to me?

MARIANE: He's only just told me.

VALÈRE: Who? Tartuffe? So that's how one gets one's way in these matters, eh? One informs the lady she's to be one's bride –

MARIANE: My father told me –

VALÈRE: Oh, excuse me, your father. Your father has just told you you're going to marry Tartuffe? Excuse me while I sort it out, it's really all a little confusing for a chap who thought he was the fiancé. Has he told my replacement yet? Does he have any views, I wonder? (*Little pause*) And do you?

MARIANE: I don't know.

VALÈRE: You don't know?

MARIANE: No.

VALÈRE: No?

MARIANE: What do *you* think I should do?

VALÈRE: Why, accept the situation, of course.

MARIANE: Are you being serious?

VALÈRE: Absolutely. Marriage only requires two consenting parties. And if Tartuffe and your father have consented, there's nothing left for you to do, or for me to say, is there? I'm sure they'll both be very happy with their choice. And you, too, no doubt.

MARIANE: I'm grateful for your advice, sir. And thank you.

VALÈRE: You won't have any trouble following it, then?

MARIANE: No more than you in giving it.

VALÈRE: I gave it to please mademoiselle. Isn't it what you wanted to hear?

MARIANE: I shall follow it to please monsieur. Isn't it what you wanted to give?

(*There is a pause.*)

DORINE: This is all going swimmingly.

VALÈRE: So this is your idea of love, is it?

MARIANE: And is this yours? Besides, what has love got to do with it? You didn't mention it when you gave me your advice. Which was that I should accept the husband that's been selected for me. I intend to follow that advice.

VALÈRE: I'm flattered. You never really loved me.

MARIANE: (*Hesitates, then tremulously*) If it pleases you to think so.

VALÈRE: Yes, yes, if it pleases me! Hah! Well, mademoiselle, shall I race you to the altar? A lady I know might be quite pleased to sprint up the aisle with me.

MARIANE: I'm sure she will. After all, the love *you* can
command –

VALÈRE: Let's just say she won't mind consoling me for what I've
lost.

MARIANE: Which is nothing much, if you can find consolation so
easily.

VALÈRE: I have a right to it, I think. A man has his pride. It
would be something of a weakness to go on loving where
there's no hope, wouldn't it?

MARIANE: How noble!

VALÈRE: Well, what would you have me do? Stand nobly by
while you throw yourself into Tartuffe's arms, and then
mope about to the end of my days? Refusing to look at any
other woman because of my undying passion, my
unquenchable love – hah – yes, I can see that might suit you.
It doesn't suit me.

MARIANE: Then, monsieur, do, by all means, what does suit you.
I wish you both every happiness. (*Curtsies*)

VALÈRE: Thank you. (*Bows*) I'll take my leave –

MARIANE: Yes, you'd better. With a marriage to arrange.

VALÈRE: (*Bows*) And yours already arranged.

(MARIANE *curtsies*. VALÈRE *bows, turns to go, comes back.*)
You've driven me to this. Please remember.

MARIANE: I shall.

VALÈRE: I'm merely following your example.

MARIANE: I'm flattered.

VALÈRE: And doing your bidding.

MARIANE: I'm grateful.

VALÈRE: So, mademoiselle, so. (*Hesitates*) We say goodbye.

MARIANE: Indeed.

VALÈRE: For ever.

MARIANE: For ever.

VALÈRE: (*Goes to the door, returns*) Mademoiselle?

MARIANE: Monsieur?

VALÈRE: You called, mademoiselle?

MARIANE: You dream, monsieur.

(*They stand looking at each other.* VALÈRE *turns to go.*)

DORINE: (*Claps*) Thank you, thank you, most enjoyable, most –
but you can stop now. Monsieur Valère (*Taking hold of his
arm*) –

VALÈRE: (*Resisting*) What do you want, Dorine?

DORINE: Come here.

VALÈRE: No – no – there's something I promised mademoiselle
there I'd do.

MARIANE: And he's in a hurry to do it. So let him go, Dorine.
(*Turns to go.*)

DORINE: No, you don't – (*Running after her, catching her arm.*)

MARIANE: What do you want, Dorine?

DORINE: Come here. And you (*Grabbing hold of* VALÈRE) – and
you (*Grabbing hold of* MARIANE) –

MARIANE: What do you want? You saw how he treated me.

VALÈRE: You heard what she said to me.

DORINE: Yes, yes, I saw, I heard, idiots, both of you. She wants
to be yours, I can vouch for it. He loves only you, I swear on
my life.

MARIANE: Then why did he tell me to marry Tartuffe?

VALÈRE: Why did she ask me whether she should?

DORINE: Yes, yes, now give me your hands. (*To* MARIANE)
Yours. Please.

MARIANE: (*Gives it*) What for?

DORINE: (*To* VALÈRE) And now yours.

VALÈRE: Why?

> (DORINE *puts their hands together. They clasp hands, as if
> unwillingly. There is a pause.* VALÈRE *looks at* MARIANE.
> MARIANE *looks down.*)

Not so much as a look!

> (MARIANE, *after a slight pause, looks at him.* VALÈRE *smiles.*
> MARIANE *smiles.* ELMIRE *enters, stands watching as* MARIANE
> *curtsies to* VALÈRE, *slowly, smiling at him.* VALÈRE *holds her
> hand still, bows to* MARIANE. *They rise, stand looking at each
> other.*)

ELMIRE: Valère.

VALÈRE: Oh – madame, excuse me, I didn't see – (*Performs a
hurried bow*) Your servant –

ELMIRE: Monsieur, you must leave this house immediately.

VALÈRE: Madame?

ELMIRE: And not return to it until you can come with honour, as my step-daughter's intended husband. And you, my child, will obey your father and agree to accept Tartuffe.

MARIANE: But, Mama —

ELMIRE: Meanwhile we'll find reasons for putting the wedding off.

DORINE: Yes – yes, madame is right, it's the only way. You can be ill sometimes, and superstitious sometimes. Bashful brides are always superstitious – you can say you broke a mirror or dreamt of muddy water or saw a corpse when you were out walking –

ELMIRE: Sooner or later my husband – your father – will recover from his – his indisposition, I know he will. Just as we all know that he is a good man, and wouldn't willingly allow harm to any of us. But you must go now –

DORINE: No – not together! Don't you understand what madame's just said – you go that way and you that –

VALÈRE: (*Goes to the door, turns to* ELMIRE) Thank you, madame. (*Bows, then looks at* MARIANE) But my best hope is (*To* MARIANE) – you, mademoiselle.

MARIANE: I promise I shall belong to no man but Valère, monsieur.
(*They look at each other.*)

DORINE: Go!
(MARIANE *and* VALÈRE *exit.*)
And how is the master now, madame?

ELMIRE: In despair. He came looking for his Tartuffe, and found only his wife. His consolation was to tell me of the marriage he had arranged. It seemed to bring him closer to Tartuffe, to imagine him in his daughter's arms. Then he went looking for him again – he thinks he might be at church, at prayer.

DORINE: Has he tried the kitchens? Or the wine cellar?

ELMIRE: I want to speak to him.

DORINE: To Tartuffe?

ELMIRE: Before my husband finds him, if possible. To dissuade him from going through with this marriage.

DORINE: Well, if anyone can, it's you, madame. I'm sure he dotes on you –

DAMIS: (*Enters*) May – may lightning strike me dead! Here, on this very spot! (*Points to the spot*) May I be for ever branded a blackguard, villain, liar, coward! If I let anything – anyone – man or devil – get between me and that – have you heard the news, madame? That I'm to acquire a brother-in-law?

ELMIRE: Yes.

DAMIS: And who it's to be, madame, who it's to be!

ELMIRE: The same man that I'll be acquiring as a son-in-law, no doubt.

DAMIS: And so goodbye to Valère. And to Valère's sister. And to the family honour. Father gave his word to Valère, how *can* he?

ELMIRE: Damis, we must be calm –

DAMIS: Calm! Calm, madame – I heard it from Laurent. The last time he was turning away our friends. Now he's turning away our fiancés.

(*There has been a sound of wailing, off.*)

DORINE: (*Goes to the door, looks out*) Madame, he's here! Tartuffe!

DAMIS: Is he? Is he, by God! Good!

ELMIRE: Now, Damis, listen to me. I'm going to try and talk to him. To see if I can dissuade him from the marriage. Do you see? So please – for everybody's sake – your own as well –

(DAMIS *hesitates*.)

TARTUFFE: (*Off*) Laurent – put away my hair shirt and lock up my scourge. Later we distribute alms to the poor wretches in prison. Pray to heaven for guidance. He will be done!

(DAMIS *hesitates*.)

ELMIRE: We must be alone.

DAMIS: Very well. (*Turns to go out.*)

(ELMIRE *turns towards the table, nods to* DORINE.)

DORINE: Monsieur Tartuffe – monsieur –

(DAMIS, *having pretended to leave, slips into one of the side rooms.*)

TARTUFFE: (*Enters. Doesn't see* ELMIRE, *who is arranging herself at the table, as* DORINE *is blocking his view*) Yes, my girl. Is your

master looking for me? He returned while I was at my
devotions, I believe.

DORINE: Yes, sir, but –

TARTUFFE: Oh, but mine eyes – mine eyes receive offence – oh,
quick, take this. (*Hands her a handkerchief*) For the love of
heaven, use it!

DORINE: Yes, sir. What on?

TARTUFFE: Your bosoms, child. The sight of them sears mine
soul. They give rise to evil thoughts.

DORINE: Really? Well, you must be easily tempted then, if a little
patch of skin does that to you. The sight of you naked from
top to toe wouldn't stir me up –

TARTUFFE: Enough, child! Enough of this – this shameful
chatter. Now where is your master?

DORINE: I don't know, sir. It's Madame Elmire who wants a
word – (*Stepping aside.*)

(TARTUFFE *sees* ELMIRE. *There is a pause.*)

TARTUFFE: (*Steps forward*) May a supremely bountiful heaven
continue to smile upon you, madame, and bless all the days
of your life with peace and joy is the desire of this its most
humble servant, and yours.

ELMIRE: How kind of you, monsieur. And pious. (*Glances at*
DORINE. DORINE *exits.*)
But let us sit down. And make ourselves comfortable.

TARTUFFE: And have you quite recovered from your little
illness?

ELMIRE: Oh, yes. Yes, the fever's quite gone. Thank you.

TARTUFFE: Can heaven have answered my prayers then? No, no
– a vainglorious thought, madame. But every cry I've cried
up to our Lord – and I've cried up – but again vainglorious,
vainglorious to count, vainglorious to say, madame – but
every cry I've cried up has been for your recovery, madame.
Your recovery. And if the Lord had demanded it, I'd have
sacrificed my own health for yours, madame, my own life.
Like Abraham and – and David, madame.

ELMIRE: Isaac, surely, monsieur.

TARTUFFE: Yes, Isaac, too, madame, and Abraham and Esau and

Rebab and Mlictan and Rebecca and (*Gestures*) – all of them, madame.

ELMIRE: Christian charity can go no further, monsieur.

TARTUFFE: Your servant, madame. Before God.

ELMIRE: And yet here we both sit, in the best of health, Monsieur Tartuffe. No sacrifices required. (*Laughs charmingly*.)

TARTUFFE: It is true that you look – you look – more than well, madame. Thanks be to – (*Lifts his eyes*.)

ELMIRE: Monsieur. (*Little pause*) I'm so glad we find ourselves alone.

TARTUFFE: For once, madame. For the first time since I came into this house. In spite of my most fervent – now at last answered me. (*Lifts his eyes*.)

ELMIRE: We can speak confidentially with each other. You will be frank with me, won't you, Monsieur Tartuffe?

TARTUFFE: Bare, madame, bare to the bottom, the very bottom, of my soul.

(ELMIRE *nods, smiles thanks*.)

I trust you understand why – during your husband's absence – I felt it necessary to put a stop to – to certain things. Your visitors, for example. It was from my concern for your religious – and moral – well-being. I wanted to – to set your soul in a cage, madame, and have it sing to God – and he would put his finger out, madame, and touch and stroke his sweet child, to make her sing so pure – so pure and clear – (*Putting his fingers out, taking hers*.)

ELMIRE: Oh! (*Smiles*) You squeeze rather – rather roughly, sir.

TARTUFFE: It is the thought of you in your (*Lifts his eyes to heaven*) – but I would never hurt you, madame. Never! How could I, when I long, so long to – do you (*Puts his hand on her knee*) – all manner of good – madame?

ELMIRE: What are you doing?

TARTUFFE: This dress, madame, made from what material – so soft – so delicate –

ELMIRE: Please. I'm – I'm rather ticklish, monsieur. (*Pushes back her chair*.)

TARTUFFE: Ticklish, ah, ticklish. (*Pushes his chair forward*) But this lace – exquisite – exquisite (*Fingering the lace at her throat*) – example of modern craftsmanship – how snugly it rests against your warm –

ELMIRE: (*Gets up*) Monsieur Tartuffe, monsieur – may I come to the point, monsieur. Can it be true that my husband is arranging a marriage between you and his daughter?

TARTUFFE: Well, madame, yes, I believe he has some such scheme, but, of course, as far as I'm concerned – (*Getting up, gesturing.*)

ELMIRE: Yes, monsieur?

TARTUFFE: My desires – my heart – my bliss – madame, lie somewhere else. I think you know where, madame.

ELMIRE: Yes, of course I do. In heaven. Your concern is for things of the spirit, not of the flesh.

TARTUFFE: Ah, madame, I am a man, with the feelings of a man. Our Lord would not have me otherwise. He who made heaven made perfections here on earth, too, through which we see his goodness shine. You are one of those, madame. Of his perfect works the most perfect. On your face he has lavished a – a beauty which dazzles mine eyes and uplifts mine soul, yea! How can I gaze on you without adoring him who made you, without mine heart contracting in love for his own divine features expressed in yours. At first I was afraid – yes, I, Tartuffe, madame, was afraid – that my growing devotion to you was a trick of the Devil. I resolved to flee from you before I was led into temptation and from temptation to destruction through and in you, but at last, madame, almost too late, ah, my most beautiful creature, I realized that I was being directed to your heart by his will, to which it is my most sacred duty to succumb. In all modesty, in humility, in the love of God – his will be done! – I offer myself to you, madame. On your reply my happiness in this world, yes, my salvation in the next, depend! In these hands (*Taking them*) – those eyes, those lips – my life and immortal soul!

ELMIRE: (*Turning away*) Should you not be more cautious, monsieur?

TARTUFFE: With what, madame? As you already have my life
and soul? (*Little pause*) You'll be safe with me, madame, I'll
guard your honour and your good name. I'm not like these
young bucks who strut about boasting of their successes –
no, no, with me, madame, you shall have love without
scandal, pleasure without fear.

ELMIRE: But if I should tell my husband what you've – offered
me, monsieur.

TARTUFFE: The fault is his. For taking to wife my – my little
temptress! (*Kneels to* ELMIRE) Stoop down, stoop down to
your unworthy salve – and with what obedience, what
devotion he will live under your spell. Ah, madame –
madame –

ELMIRE: You are lucky in your temptress, monsieur.

TARTUFFE: (*Lets out a cry of pleasure, looks up*) Madame!

ELMIRE: I shall not repeat a word of what you've said to me. But
there is a price for my discretion. You must not only
renounce any intention of marrying my step-daughter. You
must also do everything in your power to influence my
husband to honour his promise to Valère. On those terms I
shall keep secret –

DAMIS: (*Erupts from the small room*) No, madame, no! You cannot
make such a bargain! This must be made public. I overheard
it all – yes, monsieur, every word – as if God himself had
directed me – the will of heaven, monsieur – is there! (*Points*)
To show me how to destroy a hypocrite, a scoundrel and a
traitor! Hah, you're finished, Tartuffe, finished. And out of
your own mouth! Revenge is ours, madame!

ELMIRE: No, Damis, leave things as they are. I implore you.
Monsieur Tartuffe and I have reached an understanding,
have we not, monsieur? He promises to promote Mariane's
marriage to Valère, do you not, monsieur? And as I have no
inclination to be involved in a scandal – Damis, I do assure
you that we women become quite used to this sort of thing.
It's always much better not to make a fuss. Unless it's
necessary, of course. Which in this case it isn't. Is it,
monsieur?

DAMIS: I'm sorry, madame. This pest has already caused too
much misery in our house. Now we have the chance to be rid
of him – it's not only a pleasure – it's a duty – to expose him!
(*Turning to* TARTUFFE.) Well, your holiness, are you going
to stay while I do it – or skulk off like the wretched cur you
are? Ah!

ORGON: (*Off*) You say he's here – where – where?

DAMIS: Ah!

ELMIRE: Damis, I beg you, please – you'll regret it –

ORGON: (*Enters*) At last, at last, but where have you been, I've
looked everywhere for you – are you all right? You look –
what's the matter?

DAMIS: All, right! Hah! Father, I'll tell you all you need to know
about the condition of your Tartuffe. In fact he's just about
to leave our premises, but before he goes you might want a
few words with him, Father, on the subject of his attempt to
dishonour your wife! Yes, father, *that*'s how Monsieur,
Tartuffe has seen fit to repay your kindness! I need hardly
say that Madame was a most unwilling victim of his – his –
and sweet-natured as she is, not only endured it, for my sake,
and Mariane's sake, but doesn't even want me to upset you
by revealing what I – happened to witness. But I know,
Father, that I'd be doing *you* a great wrong if I failed to speak
out. I'm sorry, madame, I have no choice. It's a matter of
your honour, as well. Tell him what happened, madame.

ELMIRE: My honour has never depended on describing the
attacks that have been made on it. But on defending it
myself, with dignity and discretion. (*To* ORGON) There was
no need for you to be distressed, sir. (*To* DAMIS) I wish you'd
let yourself be guided by me. (*To* ORGON) My – apologies,
sir. (*She exits.*)

DAMIS: Well, Father, what should we do with him?

ORGON: (*Throughout has been staring at* TARTUFFE) Tartuffe – it's
not true, is it? That you would – you would – (*Shakes his
head*) Tartuffe? No.

TARTUFFE: Yes, brother, true, all true. (*Pause*) Look, brother,
upon this wicked, miserable and guilty sinner, the saddest

wretch ever to have crawled across the face of the earth. The soul of pollution, a mass of corruption, called at last to account by his God! His will be done! Oh, brother, in your righteousness – in your righteousness – drive this unclean beast from your door. I am yours! Yours – for punishment!

DAMIS: (*Laughs, applauds*) What a performance!

ORGON: (*Turning on him*) That my son – my own son!

DAMIS: What! But – but you don't believe – you can't believe this – this posturing hypocrite –

ORGON: Quiet!

TARTUFFE: No, no, brother, let him speak! Better, far better to believe him, who is your son, brother, than put your faith in me, brother . . . What am I, to have earned your faith? No, no – look first upon this, your son, whom thou lovest – and then – then look upon me and into me – and find in me what he says – your son says – is to be found, brother. Do you not see me as I am? Thief! Murderer! (*On his knees, moving from* ORGON *to* DAMIS) I bend my head! I submit unto mine enemy! (*Bends his head*) His will be done!
(DAMIS *stares down at him, lifts his fist to strike him.*)

ORGON: Noooo!
(DAMIS *lowers his fist. There is a pause.*)

DAMIS: But, Father – don't you see, can't you see, the effrontery – the sheer effrontery – (*Rallying*) Father, this creature –

ORGON: (*Roaring it out*) Hold your tongue, viper! (*Goes to* TARTUFFE) Oh, rise, brother, I beseech thee. (*Raising him up*) Oh, infamous, infamous!

DAMIS: But he's – it all –

ORGON: Silence!
(DAMIS *makes to speak.*)

ORGON: One word more, one word more – and I tear you limb from limb. With my own hands!

TARTUFFE: No, no, me! Tear *me* limb from limb, brother, with your own bare hands – but not your son, your only son – not a scratch on your only son for my sake – my life rather – (*Goes down on his knees again*) Forgive, forgive him, I implore! (*Weeping.*)

ORGON: (*To* DAMIS) See – see what you have done? Are you
satisfied? (*Little pause*) Art thou satisfied? (*In a bellow,
moving threateningly towards him.*)

DAMIS: I – I – (*Stops himself as* ORGON *comes closer.*)
(ORGON *and* DAMIS *are eyeball to eyeball. There is a pause.*)
Father.

ORGON: I know you now. All of you. My wife. My children. My
household. Know you for what you are. Jealous. Fearful.
Treacherous. Oh, wicked, wicked, wicked! But understand
– understand – my love for this – this man is stronger than
the lies and hatred; the more you struggle to harm him, the
more I shall crush you down with the full force of his
goodness.

TARTUFFE: (*As if in prayer*) His will be done.

ORGON: He enters into my family as my son. My *chosen* son.

DAMIS: You force Mariane to marry him?

ORGON: Tonight, tonight, this very night I – we – God completes
your humbling. Before heaven. I challenge you. All of you!
Who is the master? Whose will do you obey?

TARTUFFE: (*As before*) His will be done!
(*Pause.*)

ORGON: At his feet. (*Goes to* TARTUFFE, *raises him up*) At his feet!
Beg for mercy!

DAMIS: Beg for mercy! From that – that swindler! Hah!

ORGON: Do it!
(DAMIS, *after a pause, shakes his head.*)

DAMIS: (*Quietly*) But I am your son.

ORGON: A stick! A stick! I'll kill – I'll kill – (*Makes to throw
himself on* DAMIS.)

TARTUFFE: (*Holds him back*) Brother! Brother – for the love of
God! And for me, brother!

ORGON: (*Stops struggling*) Very well, very well, very well. (*Pause*)
Very well. But leave this house now, leave my house now,
never set foot in this house again. I disinherit, I curse, I – I –
this man replaces you. Your inheritance becomes his.
(DAMIS *looks at* ORGON *in horror, turns, runs off. There is a
pause.* ORGAN *stands in his rage. Then blinks, and slowly, as if*

in bewilderment turns, looks about him. Sees TARTUFFE. *There is a pause.*)

ORGON: Tartuffe – Tartuffe – my Tartuffe. (*Goes to him.*)
(TARTUFFE *opens his arms.* TARTUFFE *enfolds* ORGON *in his arms.* ORGON *lets out a wail.* TARTUFFE *strokes* ORGON'S *head.* ORGON *sinks to his knees, clutching at* TARTUFFE. *On this tableau: curtain.*)

ACT TWO

ORGON *and* TARTUFFE *are kneeling in prayer, opposite each other, and very close.* TARTUFFE, *after a moment, raises his head, looks at* ORGON, *smiles.* ORGON *seems to go on praying. Suddenly lets out a cry.*

TARTUFFE: What is it? (*Goes to* ORGON *tenderly.*)

ORGON: (*Pathetically*) I – I – oh, it's you, thank God, I – for a moment – thought I was alone. Quite alone.

TARTUFFE: How can you be alone? I am here. God is in my thoughts.

ORGON: Thank you, thank you.

TARTUFFE: But, brother, have you the strength to be alone with God, knowing that you are in my thoughts?

ORGON: What (*Looking at* TARTUFFE *fearfully.*)

TARTUFFE: Brother?

ORGON: What do you mean, brother?

TARTUFFE: I leave you, brother.

    (ORGON *cries out.*)

    Yes, brother, yes, I must. I see it now. Whether with God's grace I know not, though I've just sought his guidance, but from my crying out, 'Oh, Lord! My Lord!' I received no answering, 'Son, my son!' Sometimes his silence is our greatest test. And I lack strength.

ORGON: You – no, no. Impossible!

TARTUFFE: Oh, not in my love of him, but through my love – for you. There. I have confessed to a true sin. My love for you! I can no longer endure to suffer the spectacle of your suffering. The suffering I myself – oh, bitter, bitter! – I myself bring on you. The lies, the hatred. The jealousy. You spoke the words yourself, to your own son. All, all caused by me. But if they see you alone with our God they will understand at last that their fear is of him, not me! Their hatred, their jealousy, of him, not me. And then you may find peace. And for that I would – most willingly in spite of my heart – leave you, brother. (*Looks at him*) I remain with you in God. (*Emotionally, turns to leave*)

ORGON: No! Please, Tartuffe. (*Runs after him.*)

TARTUFFE: But while I stay their battle against you will be relentless. And one day, in the despair of their cunning, they will surely find a way to turn your heart against me.

ORGON: Never!

TARTUFFE: Oh, but brother – if you had to choose. Between me and your dearest possession, the treasure of your heart?

ORGON: (*Confused, looks at him*) But – but *you* are – are –

TARTUFFE: I mean your wife. Madame Orgon herself, monsieur.

ORGON: Oh. Well, if she loves me – how can there be a choice? If she loves me. And if you love me, how can you leave? When my life itself is at stake? If you go I – I shall lose my faith. You gave it to me. At a time when I seemed to see nothing but – but my death before me – and then you brought me light and understanding and – and my faith. Don't take it away, Tartuffe –

TARTUFFE: But then what of your wife? Am I to live as a leper in the house of mine dearest brother, demeaning you, my love for you, and our love of God, by slinking about and about the house, afraid to see her, to talk to her, because she may try again to make you turn from me in loathing? Am I? Nay, nay. (*Shakes his head*) I may not. In God's name, I may not.

ORGON: But, Tartuffe – do you think I'd listen to what she says about you? Never! Never! I would not listen to her – to anyone – to listen to them, to believe them, would mean that I'd lost my faith in you, in God, in my life – I *want* you to see her, to speak to her, in private, in public, wherever you wish, whenever you wish – I want the whole world to accuse you, lie about you, try to force me to reject you – because how else can I show my love for you, how else will you know I've made my choice. A leper! You! You, who will be my son-in-law, my brother and my master – and, yes, my sole heir. Everything I own shall be yours, legally

made over to you in due form as the world demands – and these – and these – you shall even have these. (*Taking papers out of pockets, stuffs them into Tartuffe's hands.*)
(TARTUFFE *looks at them, looks at* ORGON)
A sacred trust. Given me by my oldest friend, Argaz. He was against the king, you see, a conspirator in the uprisings – though I warned him, warned him to be loyal! Now he lives in fear, he thinks they are coming to arrest him, to search his house – so he sent for me, Tartuffe, that's why I had to leave you – to give me these, his most secret papers, some of them compromising – if they were revealed, he would be ruined, imprisoned – perhaps executed. *Now* do you see?
(TARTUFFE *stares at him, to conceal that he doesn't.*)
Now you will have everything – everything! My wife's honour, my son, my daughter, my family, my home and my dearest friend – his fate is already in your hands – and then when the world tries to reject you it also rejects me, all I am and ever was – and still we shall be as one, Tartuffe, Tartuffe, what do you say?
(TARTUFFE *turns, walks around the room, his head bent, as if in prayer.* ORGON *watches him, as if in terror.* TARTUFFE *stops, looks at* ORGON. *Pause.* TARTUFFE *puts the papers into his shirt.* ORGON *lets out a cry of joy.*)

TARTUFFE: His will be done!

ORGON: Amen, amen! I shall do the rest now – legally – in due form – this very minute – and then let the world defy us, eh, Tartuffe? Eh? (*Hurries off.*) My lawyers – my lawyers – fetch them now – now – instantly – (*Exits.*)
(TARTUFFE *stands for a moment, then spreads his arms out in exultation.* CLEANTE *enters, stares at* TARTUFFE *in amazement.* TARTUFFE, *seeing* CLEANTE, *crashes forward on to the floor, his arms still spread wide. He lies there for a moment, praying in a low mutter, then rises slowly, still praying, opens his eyes, looks at* CLEANTE.)

CLEANTE: Excuse me. I didn't mean to disturb you, but –

TARTUFFE: At monsieur's service. You entered on an act of

mortification. Your witnessing it increased my mortification.
Perhaps that was our Lord's intention.

CLEANTE: Ah, well, as a matter of fact I have an intention of my
own. Which is to discuss with you, monsieur, if I may –

TARTUFFE: Monsieur.

CLEANTE: This business of Damis. His father throwing him out
of the house and – and talking of disinheriting him. Well, as
you can imagine, monsieur, it's all over town – everybody's
talking about it. And most unfavourably, I regret to say,
monsieur, to yourself. My own view, if I may offer it, is that
whether people are being fair to you or not is really rather
beside the point.

(TARTUFFE *makes a gesture signifying martyrdom.*)

I'm perfectly willing to concede – it's only too likely – that
Damis has only himself to blame. You were doubtless the
object of one of his characteristic outbursts – in which he
quite improperly accused – indeed, is at this moment
accusing you, all over town, as I've already mentioned – and
not only improperly, but what is worse, imprudently. But
what *is* clear, monsieur, is that he believes everything he
says. Especially when saying it at the top of his voice. In the
manner of the distinguished preacher who used to note in the
margins of his sermons, 'Weak argument here, shout like
hell,' eh?

(CLEANTE *laughs. Checks his laugh as* TARTUFFE *looks
sorrowfully away.*)

Forgive me, monsieur. Unlike the distinguished preacher, I
have a tendency to misjudge my audience. I was forgetting
the – the rigorousness of your principles.

(TARTUFFE *gestures forgiveness.*)

Our concern is Damis. Whatever the shortcomings of his
temper, he is, at heart, a most honourable young man. His
slanders – as I take them to be – come from youthful
impetuosity, monsieur, rather than from malice. He would
never knowingly tell lies. (*Little pause*) You are a man of
faith, monsieur. Famously so. Could you not see your way to
– forgiving him? After all, for a Christian and an instructor in

Christ's teachings to be – however unwittingly – the cause of a loving son being driven out of his home, must give you the greatest of pain. And to be the subject of gossip and scandal can only diminish the strength of your appeal to – your public. Congregation, rather. (*Little pause*) As at the moment you appear to be the only human being – I intend you no slight, monsieur – who has the influence to reconcile my brother-in-law to his son. (*Little pause*) You can't want it to continue as it is, surely? And another thing –

TARTUFFE: (*Raises a hand*) I have forgiven him. (*Slightly intoning.*)

CLEANTE: Really? Well, that's splendid, splendid. So I can take it you'll do your best to persuade his father to re-admit him to home, family, etc.

TARTUFFE: Alas, alas.

CLEANTE: Alas?

TARTUFFE: My forgiveness is for his affront to me. But for God's forgiveness for his affront to God in slandering one of his servants is for God to give.

CLEANTE: I see. You're not at one on the matter, then? You and – (*Gestures.*)

TARTUFFE: Who can say what is in God's heart?

CLEANTE: Certainly not I. Hence my suggestion, that you intercede with his father.

TARTUFFE: But it would seem as if God has chosen not to soften the father's heart. Perhaps (*Crossing himself*) the offence is too grave.

CLEANTE: But if you would undertake to try. Use all your influence – encourage my brother-in-law to share your own condition of forgiveness, which does you so much credit, monsieur. Teach him even how to attain it?

TARTUFFE: (*Distressed*) Ah!

CLEANTE: Monsieur?

TARTUFFE: That I have done, sir. Ceaselessly taught, ceaselessly shared – but my influence over my brother, your brother-in-law, has not met with much approval in certain quarters, I believe? (*Eyeing* CLEANTE.)

113

CLEANTE: It would meet with approval in the present circumstances, sir. In every quarter. If it led to Damis being restored to his rightful place in the family. (*A little pause*) Monsieur?

TARTUFFE: I fear you mistake, monsieur, the nature of forgiveness. It is not offered instead of punishment, or to soften punishment, especially where punishment has been earned. Forgiveness and punishment flow from different sources, but work together to the same end, sir. Damis is twice blessed, in being both forgiven *and* punished for his sin. If he is truly repentant, his soul must cry out – yea, sir, cry out – for punishment. You and I may forgive him, and even his father unto his God in heaven may forgive him, yet, how – how can he forgive himself, monsieur? For his father to cast him out of his home and his inheritance is for his father to show him his love and the path to the love of the father above, who is the father of all fathers, the fount of all blessings, all forgiveness and all punishment. So let us send Damis to his salvation – by the pathways of humility.

CLEANTE: And penury?

TARTUFFE: (*Bows his head*) His will be done!

CLEANTE: And what about yourself, sir?

TARTUFFE: My – *self*, sir?

CLEANTE: Yes. Do you lord it over the home that should be his, the wealth that should be his – in righteousness? That is what the world will ask, monsieur? Is already asking?

TARTUFFE: Alas, poor world! Poor, poor world! (*Shakes his head*) And what would it say if he were to return here, sir? It would say that either he can have committed no offence, or worse – that the offence was mine! That his lies are truth and my truth – before heaven! – lies. That I am afraid of him, that he has a hold on me, that he *forced* me to have his father recall him. That would be the gossip and scandal then, monsieur, with good turned into evil, evil good, strength into weakness, weakness strength – and how would my – congregation look upon me then, sir?

CLEANTE: You'd prefer it thought you a swindler and thief.

TARTUFFE: His will be done. I accept whatever disguises God in heaven dresses me in. But whether I seem beggar, thief or saint, I am his servant. He knows – as I know, as you yourself know, of course, monsieur – that I accept the gift of the son's inheritance from the father out of my love for our God.

CLEANTE: (*After a little pause, nods*) And when you have it, you will renounce it. By passing it on to the poor and the imprisoned. As you have with all his other gifts?

TARTUFFE: Ah, monsieur, the distribution of our worldly goods – what temptations, spiritual as well as temporal! I shall have to guard myself and pray for guidance, monsieur, not to try to buy heaven's blessings by scattering away the things of the earth – which he has delivered unto me. (*Looks at* CLEANTE, *a slight smile on his lips.*)

CLEANTE: And I shall pray to God – for *justice*, sir! And decency! And retribution for vicious – scoundrels, sir!

TARTUFFE: Well, you to your prayers, monsieur. And I to mine. Unless you join me in my little room? (*Makes an ingratiating gesture*) And we worship together?

(CLEANTE *turns away.* TARTUFFE *grins at his back, turns, goes out, mumbling, head bowed.* CLEANTE *whips around, stares after him as he does so, and* TARTUFFE *exits. There is a noise outside the other door.* DORINE *enters, followed by* ELMIRE, *who is half-supporting* MARIANE.)

DORINE: Oh, it's you, sir – thank God – she's in such a state – such a state – we're frightened for her. The master's up there with the solicitors working out the settlement for her marriage to Tartuffe – surely there's something we can do – oh, think of something, monsieur!

ORGON: (*Bursts in, clutching a sheaf of papers. Stops*) Where's Tartuffe?

CLEANTE: To his little room. To pray for guidance in disposing of your –

ORGON: But I wanted him to be here, when I – I – well, anyway, here it is! (*Laughs*) They wanted me to drag it out – but I insisted – a few sentences dashed down – their signatures –

and here it is, child! A copy of your happiness, signed and sealed!

(MARIANE *says nothing*.)

Well, child What do you say?

MARIANE: Nothing, Father.

ORGON: Nothing?

MARIANE: I am your daughter?

ORGON: Ah, and so?

MARIANE: The life I have you gave me.

ORGON: And so?

MARIANE: And is yours to command.

ORGON: (*After a pause*) Is this all?

MARIANE: Yes, Father.

(*There is another pause.* ORGON *stands almost as if uncertain.*)

DORINE: No, it isn't all, how can it be all? Forbid her to marry the man she loves – force her to marry a man she loathes –

ORGON: Loathe him? Do you loathe him, child?

MARIANE: Yes, Father.

ORGON: Good. Very good. Excellent. Because the more you loathe him, the greater your virtue in surrendering to him, in obedience to me. God's will be –

DORINE: Unnatural! That's what it is –

ORGON: Hold your tongue, unless you want to follow her brother on to the street. I will purge my house. Purge it. (*Little pause*) Does anyone else wish to speak?

CLEANTE: If I may – may hazard a few words, brother –

ORGON: -in-law. Brother-in-law. Not by nature or by choice. An accident of marriage, sir. I hope that what you have to say is proper to our relationship. Otherwise – (*Gestures violently*.)

(CLEANTE *makes to speak, doesn't.*)

ELMIRE: And me? What is proper to our relationship, monsieur?

ORGON: Your husband, madame? (*Bowing slightly*.)

ELMIRE: Your wife, monsieur, believes that you have been bewitched. By a man who attempted to dishonour her.

ORGON: Well, madame, wives are prone to enjoy certain –

dramas. Even so they should make some pretence of being distressed, when they pretend to be assaulted. Out of courtesy to their husbands. Mine was too calm, madame.

ELMIRE: There are also wives, monsieur, who would pretend calm in order to save their husband's distress. Would you have believed yours more if she'd screeched like a demented prude, ravaged or otherwise? Yours thought you knew her, sir.

ORGON: He knows the man she slanders.

ELMIRE: But not the wife he married.

ORGON: I think I know them both, madame.

ELMIRE: Then test them both, monsieur, to be certain.

(*There is a slight pause.*)

Test them, monsieur. Your wife and your friend. To find out which is faithful to you.

ORGON: Hah! Ridiculous – what's the point? The affair is over – I've forgiven you your part in my son's disgrace – you've a soft heart – too lenient – but then, as a young step-mother, only to be – be expected – so – so there's nothing more to be said. Nothing.

ELMIRE: Are you afraid, then, monsieur?

ORGON: Afraid! What of?

ELMIRE: To risk your wife's virtue with your Tartuffe.

ORGON: Hah! Hah, hah!

ELMIRE: Then to risk your Tartuffe's virtue with your wife. You must be afraid of risking one or the other, must you not, monsieur? Or you would test us both. Or is it not proper to our relationship that I be allowed to prove my innocence?

ORGON: Your innocence doesn't matter. As I've already chosen to forgive you.

ELMIRE: But I choose not to be forgiven. As I have a right, instead, to your trust and my own good name. You see, monsieur, your Tartuffe is a liar, a hypocrite and a traitor.

ORGON: Madame –

ELMIRE: Or your wife is a hypocrite, a traitor and a liar. Which is the truth, monsieur? Put us to the test.

ORGON: (*After a pause*) Hah! Very well. Hah! If it will satisfy you

to – renew your – your – but what sort of test? Eh? Some trick
that you and the rest have worked out – is that it? Another of
your conspiracies – and who'll be your witness this time, do I
call Damis back, hah! Or her? Or her? Or him? Eh? Who?

ELMIRE: You, monsieur. And only you. Dorine, ask Monsieur
Tartuffe to come down, will you?

ORGON: He won't come if he's at his devotions. Not if I know my
Tartuffe.

ELMIRE: He'll come, monsieur, I stake my honour on it – if (*To*
DORINE) you tell him that his host's wife begs to see him.
(DORINE *exits*.)
(*To* MARIANE, CLEANTE) Now you must leave us, please.
This matter is now between Monsieur Tartuffe, monsieur my
husband, and myself.

CLEANTE: (*Takes* MARIANE) Come, my child. My brother-in-law
has a wife, at least. (*Looks at* ELMIRE, *smiles at her, exuent*.)

ELMIRE: Now, monsieur, if you'd help me with this table –

ORGON: What?

ELMIRE: The table – can we move it a little nearer – and adjust the
cloth – so. Thank you, monsieur.

ORGON: Hah! What nonsense –

ELMIRE: Could you get under it, please, monsieur?

ORGON: Under it! I? Under a table!

ELMIRE: But you must be in the room with us, monsieur, in case I
try to trick you and tell lies again.
(ORGON *looks at her, hesitates, gets under the table*.)

ORGON: As in a farce!

ELMIRE: Exactly, monsieur. A farce. (*Little pause*) Are you
comfortable?
(ORGON *grunts*.)
Good. Now, in order to make Monsieur Tartuffe reveal
himself, I shall have to be – not myself, monsieur. I trust that
nothing I say will shock you. Or if it does, that you wait until
Monsieur Tartuffe has had a chance to respond, before
interrupting us. After all, if he is what you know him to be, his
virtue and his love for you will protect him from me. Agreed,
sir?

ORGON: Oh, agreed – agreed, madame – but if he is what you
    know him to be – what will protect you from him? Hah!

ELMIRE: (*After a little pause*) If not my virtue, monsieur, then
    perhaps – my love for you.
    (*A slight pause*. TARTUFFE *enters, accompanied by* DORINE.)

DORINE: It's all right, madame, I didn't disturb Monsieur
    Tartuffe at his prayers, he was with the master's solicitors.

TARTUFFE: Urgent business of your husband's, madame, they
    wanted to conclude with important papers to be transferred.
    There is no situation, girl, in which the heart cannot speak
    peacefully to God.

ELMIRE: You may go, Dorine.
    (DORINE *curtsies and withdraws. There is a pause*.)

TARTUFFE: You sent for me, madame, I believe.

ELMIRE: Yes. Oh, yes. You see, monsieur, I confess I – I want
    to –

TARTUFFE: Madame?

ELMIRE: Oh, but, please – make sure no one is hiding in any of
    the rooms, listening – after what happened last time we were
    alone, monsieur, with Damis going into that dreadful frenzy.
    I was so frightened for you, monsieur, I couldn't think what
    to do except to try and calm him down. Of course I realized
    afterwards I should simply have denied everything, but it
    never occurred to me my husband would prefer to believe
    you rather than his own son – I underestimated you,
    monsieur (*Laughs*) and it doesn't matter now, does it? As
    long as no one else – are we safe then?

TARTUFFE: (*Who has been looking into the rooms, nods*) Madame?

ELMIRE: Oh, good. Then it's all worked out for the best, hasn't
    it? Damis giving us away like that means that my poor
    husband will have to go on believing in our – innocence,
    doesn't it? As long as we're careful. (*Little pause*) The
    answer, monsieur, is yes.

TARTUFFE: Yes?

ELMIRE: Surely you haven't forgotten, monsieur, that just before
    we were – interrupted, you asked me a question?

TARTUFFE: Ah.

ELMIRE: As to whether I returned your – feelings, monsieur? Have you forgotten then? Oh!

TARTUFFE: Excuse me, madame, I remember a conversation between us. But its nature was rather different from the one you appear to be describing. Certainly its conclusion –

ELMIRE: I hesitated, you mean?

TARTUFFE: You were very practical, madame. There was no hesitation.

ELMIRE: No, you're right, monsieur. Not hesitation. Prevarication. We use them equally, without conscience, when we – oh, monsieur, how little you understand a woman's heart! It wasn't my – my hesitation, prevarication, denial you should have listened to, but the shame that forced me to it.

TARTUFFE: The shame?

ELMIRE: That forced me to it. Of my – my – feelings, monsieur. I intend my refusal to be a – a promised, oh, monsieur, now you are forcing me to speak too freely, your expression, your silence, cruel, cruel. Is this how you reward me, monsieur, for listening to you with such eagerness before, thinking of you ever since – what did I say, monsieur, what did I say to deserve this, except to beg you to renounce a marriage with my step-daughter that – would have been a knife in my heart, monsieur. I was – jealous, monsieur. Is that to be condemned? I wanted you to be solely mine. Should you punish me for that? Oh, monsieur – speak – speak. For the love of God!

TARTUFFE: (*After a pause*) Forgive me, madame, but my heart, which is entirely yours, nevertheless – (*Hesitates.*)

ELMIRE: Nevertheless! Oh vile nevertheless!

TARTUFFE: – suffers still.

ELMIRE: Suffers? Your heart! Oh monsieur!

TARTUFFE: From the Devil's greatest weapon. From doubt, madame. It yearns, my heart, for confirmation. You give it hope, sweet hope. But not fulfilment. What your words have aroused, only your – charms – can satisfy. So cries out my heart, madame, yea!

ELMIRE: (*Coughing in response to a slight commotion under the table*) But, monsieur, you – you proceed so quickly. I've already gone too far, far further, than I intended – in telling you so frankly my feelings, and now, already, you would have me, oh, monsieur, have you no faith?

TARTUFFE: But how can I believe your words, though so precious to me, unless we put them to the test? Talk of love is talk, madame. While love itself is – (*Gestures.*)

ELMIRE: Oh, sir, sir – you have touched too much love in me, it troubles me, throws me into, oh, confusion, such strange confusion – oh, oh, give me time, I beseech you – time to breathe, lead me by stages, gentle stages, to submission – do not take advantage, sir, of a weakness you yourself have – have caused. Have you no charity?

TARTUFFE: Charity? But it's not I who refuse to give, madame. It is you? Why, if you love me? What are you afraid of?

ELMIRE: Of God, sir.

TARTUFFE: God?

ELMIRE: Our God in heaven, sir. About whom you've often offered to instruct me.

TARTUFFE: God in heaven will raise no serious objection to our love, madame. I assure you.

ELMIRE: But you make him sound so terrifying! When you talk of our sins and his punishment –

TARTUFFE: There will be no sin between *us*, madame, so how can there be punishment?

ELMIRE: No sin? When we betray my husband, your friend?

TARTUFFE: God looks into our intentions, madame, and, yes, our hearts! Our intentions are pure, our hearts so full of the love that flows from him, the first of all lovers, that he will look down upon us with blessings and praise. Trust me, madame, his will be done!

ELMIRE: (*Hesitantly*) But, monsieur, I don't understand –

TARTUFFE: But why do you think he gave us bodies, child, if not to join ourselves through each other in union with him? His desire is that we become one. In his name we will become one. In denying me you deny him. Oh, child, my child, you

have not listened to *my* heart, or his heart, only to the false
and easy sounds of entangling theologies and cursed pieties,
that would take us away from the heaven given to us in our
bodies by him who gives all things – that way lies blasphemy,
the Devil himself, who can be reached by wrongful
renunciation even more quickly than by – by – (*Gestures,
looks up*) If there be sin, I take it on myself, oh Lord! Know
thy son, yea! And smile on him and this your daughter in
their delight. Thy will be done! (*Looks at* ELMIRE) So come,
madame, come – he grows impatient! And so do I.
(ELMIRE, *as further commotions under the table, coughs.*)

TARTUFFE: This cough of yours, try some liquorice for it – here –
(*Gives her some.*)

ELMIRE: I think it's too late for liquorice, monsieur. (*Stops
coughing.*)

TARTUFFE: Now I've dealt with your fear of God in heaven –

ELMIRE: Yes, but – but (*Shyly*) – we live on earth, sir. In this
world of scandal and gossip –

TARTUFFE: You've forgotten what I said to you before! (*Irritably*)
I shall not speak of our affair. Nor will you, will you,
madame? And what the world doesn't know, the world can't
condemn, can it, madame? No offence in this world without
scandal, and as we'll make sure there's no scandal, we'll have
committed no offence, madame! (*Little pause, gently*) So
come, madame, come! You and I, my desire and yours, our
hearts together, God and nature, all insist – that you yield,
madame. So come, madame, come (*Almost crooning*) come,
madame, come (*Taking her by the hand, raising her up, turning
to face her*) – come, madame, come –
(ELMIRE *coughs again.*)

TARTUFFE: (*Starts with irritation and, more sharply*) Come,
madame, come!

ELMIRE: Oh – oh – (*Recovering herself*) Well, monsieur, I see – I
see I must. Wherever you take me, monsieur. How can I
refuse you when you won't be satisfied with less than
everything I can give? And yet it's hard – or so it seems – that
the words of women mean so little to men who swear love to

them, that we must either be distrusted or put to the test.
But I am forced to this – this extremity, monsieur, am I not?
The fault is not in me, sir, I pray?

TARTUFFE: What fault there is, madame, is mine alone. (*Taking
her in his arms*) I've already said, I take it on myself –

ORGON: (*Coming out from under the table*) No, wretch, the fault is
mine, you shall not rob me of that! (*To* ELMIRE) My fault,
my lady, to have forced you to this – this extremity. (*Turns to*
TARTUFFE) Well, my – my passionate swain, my loving
shepherd! Marry my daughter and sleep with my wife, and
both with God's blessing, eh? What a spoiled darling of
heaven you are. Oh, traitor, villain, liar, oh! (*Stops, looks at
him, and quite simply*) You were my brother, Tartuffe, I loved
you.

TARTUFFE: I still am. You still do. This – lady here –

ORGON: Don't, don't, don't – speak!

TARTUFFE: I knew you were there. I was merely attempting to
show – yes, before the eyes of the Lord –

ORGON: Don't!

(TARTUFFE *begins to mumble a prayer, eyes closed, head
bowed.*)

Stop. Stop! (*Almost strikes him*) Never! Never! Never again,
never! Leave. Leave now. For your own sake, and without
harm. To punish me for my folly – leave now.

TARTUFFE: (*Blandly*) Leave where, monsieur?

ORGON: My house.

TARTUFFE: Most willingly, monsieur. If you had a house for me
to leave. But surely even you, monsieur, swollen with
hypocrisy at the side of your (*Snarling, to* ELMIRE) –
treacherous (*Back to* ORGON) – wife, monsieur, can scarcely
order me off my own property, can he, madame? So
(*Continuing to* ELMIRE) – you found a sin to commit after all?
Well, punishment follows, just as you feared. (*To* ORGON)
This will be done? (TARTUFFE *exits.*)

ELMIRE: What does he mean?

(ORGON *stares hopelessly after* TARTUFFE.)

Tell me (*Little pause*) – husband –

ORGON: The deed of gift.

CLEANTE: (*Enters*) Well, he's gone. (*Triumphantly*) So I take it –
(*Stops, seeing their expressions.*)

ELMIRE: The deed of gift?

ORGON: The deed of gift. Signed, sealed and everything I – we –
had is his.

CLEANTE: Everything?

ORGON: Everything.

CLEANTE: And he proved himself to be –

ORGON: Everything. Everything my – my wife – you said – you
all said – ruined, ruined because of – because of – my – my –

CLEANTE: Yes, but still, we must keep calm. Calm above all.
Now first, first, we find out whether this deed can be legally
rescinded. And if it can't, reflect on consolations. You've
rediscovered your wife and your wits in even less time than it
took you to lose your home, your fortune and your son.
Monsieur Tartuffe's connection with heaven certainly seems
to give him the power to speed events along –

ORGON: Oh!

ELMIRE: Brother!

CLEANTE: Yes, I'm sorry. My tendency to misjudge –

ORGON: No, no, you're right – I deserve everything – everything
– but, by God! The next time I clap eyes on some penniless
vagabond in church I'll – I'll crush him, stamp on him, spit
on him –

CLEANTE: In church? Well, don't reform yourself too zealously –
you know, if you have a weakness – (*Catches* ELMIRE's *eye*)
But the question is, remains, what to do to retrieve your
property, and, incidentally, your son and your daughter –
and I must say, given that you appear to have – have – I
counsel prudence. Let's not go at him directly, we're bound
to lose. So, brother, I suggest we – um – we –
(DAMIS *enters, followed by* MARIANE *and* DORINE.)

DAMIS: Is it true, Father, is it? That this – this scoundrel – this
shameless and cowardly and – this – ungrateful –

ORGON: Yes.

DAMIS: What?

ORGON: True.

DAMIS: Ah. Ah! Then leave him to me! I'll deal with him, I'll get rid of him, I'll – I'll take him by the throat and I'll – I'll – (*Gestures.*)

ORGON: (*Wryly*) *My* son.

DAMIS: Father, oh, Father –
(*They embrace.*)

ORGON: And my daughter.
(*They embrace.*)

CLEANTE: Well, you see, you've already recovered wife, son and daughter with no palpable effort –

MME PERNELLE: (*Enters*) What's all this?

ORGON: Mother?

MME PERNELLE: These stories going around.

ORGON: Ah! Well, Mother, I took him in out of (*Hesitates slightly*) – charity, clothed him, fed him, looked after him as if he were my own brother. Gave him my daughter's hand in marriage, threw my son out of the house for his sake, then made over to him everything I possess. His response has been to attempt to appropriate my wife, and when I object, to drive us all on to the streets. Are those the stories going around?

MME PERNELLE: Who?

ORGON: Monsieur Tartuffe, Mother.

DORINE: (*Sotto*) The poor chap.
(ORGON *turns, as if to glare at her, smiles instead.*)

MME PERNELLE: Nonsense!

ORGON: Thank you, Mother.

MME PERNELLE: They say it out of envy.

ORGON: Of whom, Mother?

MME PERNELLE: Of Monsieur Tartuffe, of course.

ORGON: Ah. And what do I say it out of? Although it's true I envy him my house, my lands –

MME PERNELLE: When you were a child, my child, I told you again and again that virtue is for ever persecuted in this world, that though the wicked die, wickedness itself lives on, flourishing always.

ORGON: And you were right, Mother. I've seen my wife's, my son's and my daughter's persecution myself. And Monsieur Tartuffe flourishes.

MME PERNELLE: Monsieur Tartuffe would never do anything wicked.

ORGON: (*Bellowing*) Mother – Mother –

ELMIRE: (*Calming him with her hand*) Husband, husband.
(ORGON *looks at* ELMIRE, *controls himself.*)

MME PERNELLE: Earthly appearances are deceptive, good seems like bad, bad like good – Monsieur Tartuffe has his motives.

ORGON: To own my property, marry my daughter, make love to my wife – those are his motives, Mother! For God's sake –
(ELMIRE *again controls him with a touch.*)

CLEANTE: Can we get back to the main problem? How to deal with him.

DAMIS: I agree.

CLEANTE: As I was suggesting before. We must compromise.

DAMIS: I disagree! Compromise with that – that – thief and – and – (*Gestures*) Everybody knows what he's done, how he's tricked and taken advantage of an (*Looks at his father*) – um, us. They'll take our side, they're bound to! Aren't they?

CLEANTE: Some. Others will celebrate your disaster. Everybody will enjoy the ensuing controversy. Nothing either party says will affect the facts. We are the suppliants now. And as such, I really do suggest we –

ORGON: Argaz!
(*There is a pause.*)

CLEANTE: What?

ORGON: (*Suddenly frantic*) Oh, my God, oh, my God, what have I done, Argaz, what have I done to you?
(*Goes to* ELMIRE.)
You see, you see, even though I've got you back – all of you – God is making a sacrifice, I am still to be an instrument of destruction, but that it should be Argaz, my Argaz – oh, I pray, I pray he hasn't thought –
(LOYAL *enters during this, coughs for attention.*)
What? Who is that man, send him away! Dorine –

DORINE: (*Going to* LOYAL) My master is in conference.

LOYAL: Then, mademoiselle, I've no desire to intrude. But assure your master that my presence will not distress him. On the contrary, I am here to discharge the responsibility of telling him (*Pauses*) – something he will want to hear, mademoiselle.

ORGON: (*Calling*) What?

DORINE: What? Who are you?

LOYAL: The embodiment of Monsieur Tartuffe's most generous impulses. (*Bowing deeply*.)

DORINE: Master, he comes from Tartuffe. He says you'll want to talk to him.

CLEANTE: See him! You must! Perhaps he's offering a reconciliation –

(ORGON *hesitates, looks at* ELMIRE. ELMIRE *smiles, nods support*.)

ORGON: Monsieur?

LOYAL: (*Sweeping himself forward*) Your servant, sir. And may heaven strike down those who wish you harm. Furthermore, may she favour you, sir, and those connected to you (*Bowing in general direction of others*) – all the days of your life.

ORGON: Thank you. (*Bows slightly*.)

(LOYAL *offers himself for inspection and recognition*.)

(*Confused*) Um – well, please continue. If you have something –

LOYAL: You don't recognize me, then?

ORGON: No. No, I'm afraid – um –

LOYAL: I was your father's servant, sir. This house has always been most dear to me.

ORGON: Oh, forgive me, monsieur, forgive me. Circumstances at the moment, you understand – and – and what is your name?

LOYAL: Loyal.

ORGON: Loyal. Well that's certainly a fine name, a fine name, eh? (*Looking around optimistically*.)

LOYAL: I'm a native of Normandy, monsieur, as perhaps your father mentioned. Since leaving his service I've risen somewhat in the world. (*Little pause*) I am now a tipstaff.

ORGON: What?

LOYAL: A tipstaff, monsieur. And now here I am, back in the old home of my dead master, to serve a writ on his son. Isn't that a consummate irony, monsieur?

ORGON: Did you hear – did you hear –

LOYAL: Now calm, sir, calm. My writ is merely a summons to have you and yours remove yourselves, from this house, along with such approved personal items to which you may still have claim, without delay or remission, as hereby decreed, to make way for the legally established owner. That's all, sir.

ORGON: To leave this house –

LOYAL: If you would be so kind, monsieur. At the moment you happen to be trespassing on the property of one Monsieur Tartuffe. I have the documents. They are in good order. As one would expect, monsieur, as they are signed by yourself, and witnessed by your own solicitors.

DAMIS: (*Laughs noisily*) Well, I must say, I admire his impudence. (*Advancing*) Good God man –

LOYAL: (*Sharply*) My business is not with you, boy! (*Turns to* ORGON) It is with you, sir. Whom I know to be – in as much as you resemble your father – a reasonable and civil man, with a reverence for the law and a strong sense of justice. This being the case, you'll allow me to discharge my responsibilities by delivering the papers, and clearing the premises. Nothing but the items currently in your pockets to go with you is, of course, understood, sir.

DORINE: And your name is Loyal, is it?

LOYAL: I sympathize with you, I need hardly say. I wouldn't have burdened myself with this melancholy duty if I hadn't feared the alternative might be a colleague with no sentimental attachment to – (*Gestures around.*)

CLEANTE: – the prospect of throwing us on to the streets.

LOYAL: Monsieur, there is no question of throwing you anywhere. I insist that you take your time. Indeed, I will suspend proceedings until tomorrow morning. During the night ten of my men will occupy the premises with the

minimum of fuss and scandal, and in return for this
concession you will deliver over – a formality, you
understand, sir – the keys to all the doors of Monsieur
Tartuffe's house before you go to bed. And then, after a good
night's sleep – I shall personally see to it that you're not
disturbed – you'll clear the house. I shall put my men at your
disposal – strong fellows all, I chose them personally, with
you in mind. Given so much consideration on my part,
monsieur, I am sure you, on yours, will treat me as I deserve
– (*Bowing.*)

ORGON: As you deserve! Yes, yes, I'll treat you as you deserve – a
stick, a stick – where's my stick –

CLEANTE: Calm down, calm down –

DAMIS: No, no – the stick – get the stick – let me be the one –

DORINE: And me! I'll lay about you –

CLEANTE: Enough, enough of this! Monsieur Loyal, serve your
writ, for God's sake, and leave us.

LOYAL: Thank you, monsieur. And please do not be embarrassed
when you come to recollect your behaviour, monsieur. I
assure you that the ability to endure such demonstrations is a
chief qualification in my profession. (*Bows.*) May heaven
preserve you all in happiness and health.

ORGON: (*As* LOYAL *exits*) May it confound you and him who sent
you!
(*There is a long silence.*)
Ah, well – and what are your views now, Mother, on the
deception of earthly appearances and good being bad and
bad good? Which is this, Mother?

MME PERNELLE: I don't believe it! I can't believe it! I won't
believe it!

CLEANTE: Then you have an advantage over the rest of us,
madame.

DORINE: Perhaps madame thinks that Monsieur Tartuffe is
concerned for our souls. Riches corrupt. Out of charity he
taketh them away from us. Salvation is ours - yes!

ORGON: Yes, thank you, Dorine, enough – enough –
(ELMIRE *goes to him to comfort him. There is a pause.*)

DAMIS: If only – if only – (*Subsides.*)
    (*There is a pause.*)

CLEANTE: Well –
    (*There is a pause.*)

VALÈRE: (*Enters*) Excuse me, monsieur – madame – (*Looks at* MARIANE) mademoiselle – excuse me – only a matter of the greatest urgency would have brought me here at such a time – and knowing myself to be so unwelcome.

ORGON: In other words, more bad news.

VALÈRE: A close friend, a member of the court, trusted by the king and privy to the affairs of state has just warned me that you are in danger, sir.

ORGON: Yes.

VALÈRE: Your friend – Tartuffe – has just brought charges against you. He has in his possession the private papers of a most compromising kind belonging to –

ORGON: Oh, God, have I betrayed Argaz, then?

VALÈRE: And Tartuffe claims that you assisted in the concealment of these papers. He says he obtained them from you by means of a trick – in the king's name. It would seem that your friend will be arrested, monsieur. And that there is a warrant out against you. Tartuffe himself has undertaken to place you in custody. He is on his way now, with a police officer from the king himself following. They'll be here any minute, monsieur.

ORGON: Thank you.

VALÈRE: My coach is at the door. I've brought a thousand louis. Take them – please, please – (*Forcing them into* ORGON's *hands*) We must leave now, at once.

ORGON: We?

VALÈRE: I can help you –

ORGON: Valère – my son, as I believe you once wished to be. Here (*Takes him by the arm*) is my daughter, Mariane. Here, my child, is Valère. Whatever plans you have, make them between you. Here is your journey –

CLEANTE: Yes, but the carriage for yours is outside. Could you get into it –

ORGON: For what? My journey? But I've made my journey. When I began I had a wife and family, on my way I met Tartuffe and tried to give my wife and family away. Instead I gave away my home, betrayed my dearest friend and will lose my freedom – my journey is complete when I join Argaz in prison. I owe him that. His will be done.

ELMIRE: Husband, please! You must escape. For all of us.

ORGON: (*Looks at her, nods, turns to* VALÈRE) Well –

TARTUFFE: (*Enters with* LAURENT. *To* ORGON, ELMIRE, MARIANE, DAMIS, VALÈRE, CLEANTE, DORINE) Ah, monsieur, madame, mademoiselle, monsieur, monsieur, monsieur, mademoiselle – Take up your position, Laurent. (LAURENT *goes to stand by* ORGON) I bring greetings and blessings from our king, long may he reign over us in wisdom and power – but you appear a little restrained, monsieur, not your usual warm, excitable self – is it perhaps because you've been turned out of your lodgings? Well, don't worry, our royal majesty, who has the interests of all his subjects at heart, has enabled me, through his mercy, to place at your disposal – a small room, in one of his jails. There to rest while waiting his judgement. Ah – (POLICE OFFICER *enters, accompanied by several men.*)

TARTUFFE: Here is one of his officers, to escort you to your new accommodation. Execute your warrant, monsieur. His will be done. His will be done.

POLICE OFFICER: His will be done. This warrant has been too long in the execution. Justice awaits you. Seize him, Laurent.
(LAURENT *seizes* TARTUFFE.)

TARTUFFE: Monsieur? (*Struggling*) Sir? Me, sir?

POLICE OFFICER: You, sir.

TARTUFFE: Hah? And why, sir?

POLICE OFFICER: Do you not know me?

TARTUFFE: Know you? An officer sent to do his duty? What more should I know of you?

POLICE OFFICER: That I am the law.

TARTUFFE: Then do the duty of the law.

POLICE OFFICER: The law is doing its duty. (*Steps forward. His cloak falls open*)
(*There is music.* TARTUFFE *stands in the grip of* LAURENT, *staring at the* POLICE OFFICER, *who is, of course, King Louis XIV. All the others kneel.* POLICE OFFICER *extends his hand.* ORGON *kisses it.* TARTUFFE *is forced to his knees. Throws back his head in a grimace, as if in a silent howl. Music continues. Curtain.*)